Transforming THE Intense Child

WORKBOOK

AN EXPERIENTIAL GUIDE FOR PARENTS, EDUCATORS AND THERAPISTS FOR LEARNING AND IMPLEMENTING THE NURTURED HEART APPROACH

BY HOWARD GLASSER with *MELISSA LOWENSTEIN*

Transforming THE IntenseChild WORKBOOK

**AN EXPERIENTIAL GUIDE FOR LEARNING AND IMPLEMENTING
THE NURTURED HEART APPROACH FOR PARENTS, EDUCATORS & THERAPISTS**

Copyright 2016 by Nurtured Heart Publications

The Nurtured Heart Approach is a trademark of Nurtured Heart Publications.
For information contact:

Nurtured Heart Publications
4165 West Ironwood Hill Drive
Tucson, Arizona 85745
E-mail: adhddoc@theriver.com

For information about bulk purchasing discounts of this book or other Nurtured Heart Approach books, CDs or DVDs and for orders within the book industry,
please contact Brigham Distributing at 435-723-6611.

Cover Art by Alice Glasser
Cover Design and Book Design by Owen DeLeon
Owen Visual Communication

Editing by Melissa Lynn Lowenstein

Prolong Press Limited –Hong Kong

Library of Congress Card Catalogue Number: Pending

ISBN 978-0-9826714-8-1

Printed in China
First Printing: December 2016
2023 Revision

Table of Contents

Introduction:
ABOUT THIS BOOK

CHAPTER OBJECTIVES

Through Amanda's story, develop a basic understanding of the difference between traditional discipline and the Nurtured Heart Approach. Making success inevitable by seeing success in "baby steps."

One fine morning, a child opens her eyes to a new day.

She lies snug in her warm bed, taking a few extra moments to marshal her energy. As her eyes drift closed for a last little snooze, she hears her mother's voice through the doorway to her room.

"Amanda!" she says stridently. "Sweetheart. You need to get up right now. I don't like having to harass you all morning just to get you out the door in time."

Amanda sighs. "Okay, Mom," she says, and by the time she clambers out of bed, Mom has rushed off to her next task. She does her usual morning routine: brushes her teeth and hair, gets into her clothes, gets herself to the breakfast table and pours herself a bowl of cereal. As she eats, her parents rush around, trying to get everyone out the door on time.

"Could you eat that cereal any more slowly?" asks Amanda's father. "Come on – it's gonna be soggy by the time you finish it, and you're not getting anything else to eat."

"Amanda, love, you have to pack up your backpack," says Mom. "Just please hustle. Amazing – in school you can't sit still and focus for three minutes at a time, but when we really want you to move it, you sure can move slow," she says, giggling and giving her a little squeeze.

And so it goes. By the time they leave the house, Amanda has been subjected to critiques about her clothes ("There's a hole in those jeans. Don't you care how you look?"), her bed-making abilities ("You call that bed *made*? Oh, Amanda...."), her follow-through ("Amanda! I've told you twice now to get your shoes on and you keep getting distracted. Focus, please!") and, finally, her attitude ("Don't you use that tone of voice with me, young lady. You can leave that bad attitude behind you this instant").

These parents aren't mean. They are loving. They hug her and tell her they love her, often. They try to be positive by complimenting her when she does something well. But those compliments are far fewer in number and far lower in intensity than the negative statements she receives. Her parents want to teach her to follow the rules and to behave admirably, and they think spotting and commenting on areas where Amanda is falling short is the best way to achieve this. This is how their own parents raised them, more or less, and look – they turned out pretty good.

Amanda finally gets out of her mom's car at school and heads in. At school, her experience isn't all that different. Her teachers don't seem to notice her unless she screws up, loses focus, or misbehaves. She's not an excellent student – they've said she might have ADHD, because she has trouble sitting still and staying focused – but she does okay, and usually she does her best. But for every word of approval or support she hears from her teachers,

there's at least two statements about how she could do better or how she's falling short. When praise comes, it's typically some muted form of "thank you" or "good job," but when criticism or reprimands arise, the adults wax poetic, using language full of vivid, energized detail.

On this day, as she has on many other days, Amanda starts to feel something like an ache in her guts and chest. It's not pain, exactly; it feels more like something is missing. She wants something, but she doesn't really know what it is, and all she can seem to do to help stop that feeling from gnawing at her is act out. She approaches rule boundaries, then breaks them, and for the moment, all the adults around her really show up. They might be mad, and they might be criticizing her or punishing her, but at least they are seeing and connecting with her. The ache subsides, but only temporarily. As soon as she's "good" again, the adults around her stop showing up; their attention snaps back to the busyness of their lives. Once again, she feels invisible.

She notices how much more lit up the adults get with kids who misbehave more than she does. Without meaning to, or even really wanting to, she begins to follow their lead. She gets in trouble more and more. Consequences escalate. Parents and teachers begin to feel helpless and afraid when she is around. What might she do next? Which boundary might she push today? Most of us know that it only takes one challenging kid to up-end a classroom or a family, and Amanda is on her way to becoming that kid.

Soon enough, Amanda's parents and teachers decide it's time for her to see a doctor. Maybe if she receives an official ADHD diagnosis, she can try taking medication that will help keep her in line and on task.

Now, let's rewind Amanda's day and let it play out in an entirely new paradigm – the paradigm in which you will be immersed as you make your way through this workbook.

In this version of the story, Amanda opens her eyes to a new day and lies snug in her warm bed for a few extra winks, and her mother comes in to see her still cozied up under the covers.

"Amanda!" she says, brightly. "I can see you're already awake, right on schedule, and I can see you're getting your body ready for the shock of the cold morning air in here! I appreciate how you're clearly trying to stay on schedule and make it to school on time." She takes a few seconds to go to her, rub her back briskly, and start to peel back the covers. "Oooh! Chilly air. Thanks for not fighting me on this – it's fun to help you get up in the morning when you cooperate so beautifully."

Amanda's not happy to get up, but she sighs, "Okay, Mom," and clambers out of bed.

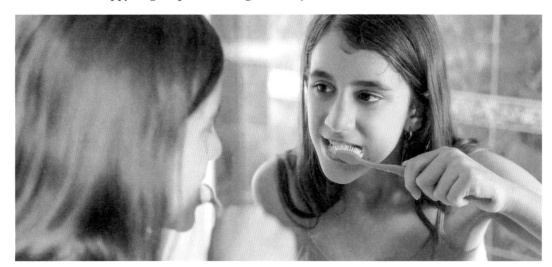

"I see you on your feet and ready to start your day," Mom says, "That's showing me that you have the greatness of internal motivation. See you down at the breakfast table!"

Amanda dives into her morning routine: brushes her teeth and hair, gets into her clothes, gets herself to the breakfast table and pours herself a bowl of cereal. Wherever Mom or Dad's paths cross with hers, they make positive comments about what she's doing well, what she isn't doing wrong, and how all her choices reflect the great qualities she carries around inside, all the time. She feels good about how she's brushed her hair, gotten her outfit together, and packed up her things, because her parents have learned how to find the miraculous and great within even her very smallest positive choices. As those small positive choices are celebrated, Amanda feels drawn to make more such choices.

Even in this atmosphere of positivity, things go wrong. Amanda is eating breakfast too slowly. They're starting to run late. Amanda's dad sits down across from his daughter and says, "Amanda, I need you to eat a little more quickly so we can get everyone out the door on time."

"I'm eating as fast as I can," says Amanda, crossly. "Stop bugging me."

Dad calmly says, "Amanda, reset." Amanda says, "Geez…" under her breath and keeps eating in silence as Dad looks over his day's calendar on his smartphone. A few seconds later, Dad looks up, focuses completely on Amanda, and says, "Thanks for taking that moment to reset. I appreciate that you're not speaking rudely to anyone right now, and I see you're doing all you can to finish breakfast in time to leave at 8 am sharp. Carry on."

And so it goes. By the time they leave the house, Amanda has been subjected not to critiques, but to detailed appreciative statements. When she gets out of her mom's car at school and heads in, she's feeling seen, acknowledged, connected with and honored for just being who she is and doing what's required.

Ideally, her experience in school is the same. If teachers, administrators and other school staff have learned the approach Amanda's parents have learned, they are equally intent upon giving their energy to what's going well and to giving a simple "reset" and welcome-back when things start to go wrong. They do this with every student and with each other. Whether Amanda has ADHD or not, or falls into some other classification of the "difficult" or "challenging" child, she has the benefit of being seen for her strengths and

for all the moments where she is doing absolutely nothing wrong – which, for even the most terrifyingly intense child, is actually most of the time. In our culture, we've become so accustomed to seeing and commenting on what's not great. What children like Amanda really respond to, however, is being acknowledged during moments when "not-great" *isn't* happening – in other words, when greatness is seen and appreciated.

In this scenario, Amanda's parents and teachers have both learned to avoid accidentally worsening negative behavior by reacting to it strongly. Now, they consistently, strongly refuse to give an ounce of their energy or a shred of relationship to negativity, while still providing an effective form of accountability that they apply the second a rule is broken.

Unlike the Amanda in the first version of this story, this Amanda does not feel an ache or an emptiness around the way adults interact with and support her. She feels full. She feels safe. And from this space of fullness and safety, she can learn well and interact with peers in mostly constructive, intelligent ways. And she can feel connected and invigorated without the rush of challenging adult authority or breaking rules. When things go awry, she gets a simple reset and lots of connection for getting back on task.

The adults around her feel the same fullness and safety. Amanda's parents and the staff of her school no longer fear children's rule-breaking or oppositional behaviors. They have a set of tools that enables them to support even the most challenging child into living out his or her greatness.

These tools do not require any more time or effort than the persistent and less-than-effective nagging, cajoling or lecturing these adults once relied upon. In using these tools with the children in their care, these adults end up being transformed themselves: into people who automatically look for the great in themselves and others. They choose to give their energy to greatness, because that is what they truly love and want to help grow.

Collectively, these tools are known as the Nurtured Heart Approach, and they are the subject of this book. Welcome, and congratulations. You're about to experience transformation.

This book will introduce you to the Nurtured Heart Approach, an approach to parenting and working with children, that is, at its foundation, about promoting positive relationship through simple (if, initially, counter-intuitive) practices.

The Nurtured Heart Approach is more than just a parenting or behavior-management strategy; it is a philosophy for creating healthy relationships. It was developed to guide intense or difficult children into their own greatness, but has proven highly effective for all children. The approach is about capturing everyday moments truthfully and reflecting them back to children in ways that celebrate great decisions, judgment and wisdom. It is about gently but steadfastly refusing to give energy to negative behaviors while never failing to enforce rules in a simple, powerfully effective way.

THE NURTURED HEART APPROACH IS ABOUT CAPTURING EVERYDAY MOMENTS TRUTHFULLY AND REFLECTING THEM BACK TO CHILDREN IN WAYS THAT CELEBRATE GREAT DECISIONS, JUDGMENT AND WISDOM.

Although this approach is as close to a magic fix-all as any we've seen, we can't guarantee that learning and using it will be easy or smooth. Like anything worth knowing or doing, the NHA can challenge you to your core. It requires practice, commitment and follow-through. It requires an intention not only to change the behaviors of children in your care, but to transform your own ways of relating to them – ways that likely are rooted in the entirety of your own life experience relating to others.

The rewards make the work worthwhile. This approach will equip you with all you need to restore positive relationship with the children in your world. If you've lost that in those relationships, you know how *not-great* it is when it slips away. How great will it be to have that gift back?

This approach has proved useful for parents, educators, and therapists who wish to move a challenging child into greatness. As you move through this book, you may find references that will make the approach more useful for your particular role, but overall, the gist of the approach will be the same across the board.

If you already have strongly positive relationships with the children in your world, know that there is almost no limit to the potential for its expansion, and that you hold in your hands the gateway into the fullness of that potential.

Welcome to Transformation
AN INTRODUCTION TO THE NURTURED HEART APPROACH

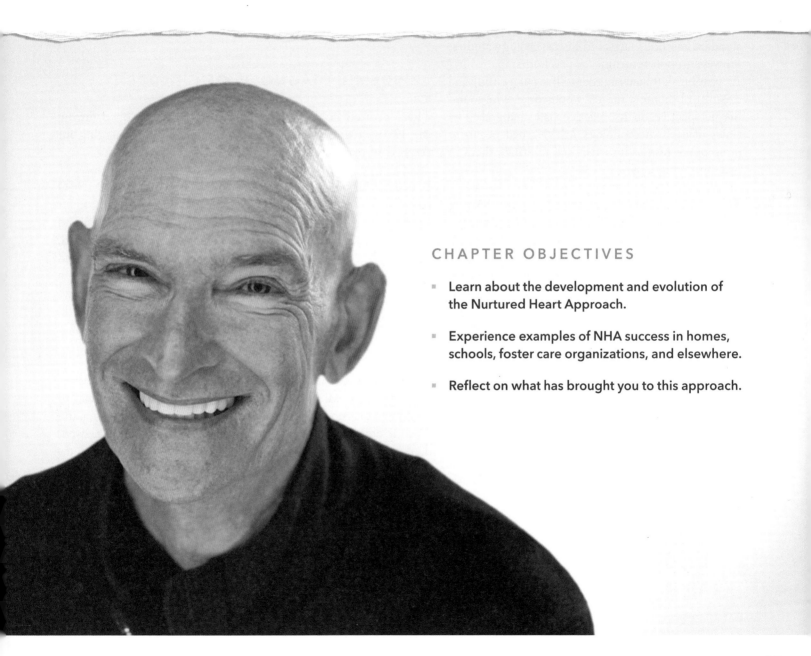

CHAPTER OBJECTIVES

- Learn about the development and evolution of the Nurtured Heart Approach.

- Experience examples of NHA success in homes, schools, foster care organizations, and elsewhere.

- Reflect on what has brought you to this approach.

Howard Glasser was stumped.

A passionate NYU-educated psychotherapist who had trained intensively to help people in difficult times of their lives, he was finding that the tools he'd studied so diligently during his education were failing him. As a student, he had been loyal to the standard methods taught in his psychology studies. However, upon returning to psychotherapy from a 15-year break (taken in order to live out a childhood dream to become a master woodworker), he found his perspective on its practice had changed. The flaws of each methodology he'd learned began to jump out at him as he attempted to utilize them in real-time situations.

These philosophies and practices were not helping the children and families he was now being trusted to help. They often seemed to make things worse. More intensely applying these methods seemed to make problems worse yet. Families were in crisis. They were clearly trying as hard as they could with the tools they had and consistently coming up short. Children were sometimes even endangering themselves and others. Schools were trying their best to handle these children, without much success. And in droves, kids were being diagnosed and labeled as mentally ill and put on powerful psychiatric medications in an attempt to control them at home and in school.

EPIDEMIC DIAGNOSIS OF CHILDREN

The Nurtured Heart Approach was initially developed during the 1990s, a time during which diagnoses of and drugging for ADHD were skyrocketing.

Between the years of 1980 and 2007, prevalence of ADHD diagnosis rose eightfold. Prescribing of stimulant drugs for children with ADHD quadrupled between 1987 and 1996 and would continue to rise almost 10 percent more by 2005.[1] Howard, along with a great many experts in the field of psychology and psychiatry, saw that these medications were a stopgap, not a solution: that they might "improve" the child's behavior and ability to focus in the short term, but did nothing to help the child learn to manage intensity.

One concern bothered Howard even more than prospective physical side effects like stunted growth, loss of appetite, heart problems, insomnia, or medication-caused behaviors that began to lead to additional diagnoses and drugs: he suspected that diagnosing and labeling children would set them up to see themselves as flawed, damaged, or handicapped. He was most troubled by the meta-message medications sent to the child: *something is wrong with your natural level of intensity. You can't handle it, nor can the adults in your life, and we need to make it go away.*

---

[1] http://www.psychiatrictimes.com/adhd/problems-overdiagnosis-and-overprescribing-adhd/page/0/1

IS INTENSITY THE ENEMY?

Think of a child who has challenged you to your core: a child who breaks rules, pushes boundaries, and escalates. Think of a child with whom nothing seems to work to keep him or her in line, on task, or inspired; with whom any attempt at consequences, warnings, or punishments might lead to at most a temporary lull, but then rolls into some even greater variation on the theme of being difficult. Life with the child feels like an edge-of-your-seat suspense story: when will the next problem arise and how will you deal with it this time? The anxiety and fear can feel overwhelming.

What adjectives would come to mind were you to attempt to describe that child? "Difficult?" "Bad?" "Defiant?" "Oppositional?" "Challenging?" If you're more committed to a positive slant, your initial attempt to come up with defining words might be more along the lines of "spirited," or "sensitive," or "energetic."

The term Glasser has carefully chosen to refer to this kind of child is *intense*. A child who is intense is like a car with a Ferrari engine and old model-T Ford brakes: the braking system isn't adequate to handle the engine's power and drive.

THE INTENSE CHILD IS LIKE A CAR WITH A FERRARI ENGINE AND OLD MODEL-T FORD BRAKES: THE BRAKING SYSTEM ISN'T ADEQUATE TO HANDLE THE ENGINE'S POWER AND DRIVE.

Intensity is not bad. It is life force. It drives all of us. We wouldn't be able to accomplish a thing without it. It powers and empowers life. It fuels our dreams and passions. Without it, we might not even be able to get out of bed. And some of us simply have more intensity than others.

Children with a normal level of intensity may respond to traditional modes of discipline. The fear of consequences or of "being bad" are often enough to keep children with moderate intensity within the boundaries of rules. A child with greater intensity is a different story. For such a child, conventional methods will usually make the situation *worse*.

Many of the "symptoms" labeled as pathology in children are really about an abundance of physical and emotional intensity that the child has not yet learned to handle.

MANY OF THE "SYMPTOMS" LABELED AS PATHOLOGY IN CHILDREN ARE REALLY ABOUT AN ABUNDANCE OF PHYSICAL AND EMOTIONAL INTENSITY THAT THE CHILD HAS NOT YET LEARNED TO HANDLE.

Consider This...

1. Consider your own intensity. What are its gifts? What are its challenges?

2. Now, consider the child or children on whose behalf you are learning this approach. If you re-frame their challenging behaviors as an expression of their intensity, how does that help you see that child or children in a new light? How might that intensity empower that child's character and contributions as we convert that very same energy that's gone awry into greatness?

Like Peter Breggin, MD, and a handful of other experts, Howard came to believe that what the medical/psychiatric mainstream was calling a "disorder" was actually something that could be seen as a gift and channeled into greatness. And he knew that a new understanding of intensity was the key that would unlock new ways of working with so-called "challenging children."

As Howard's frustration peaked, he began to have glimmers of insight into how he might better be able to support these children at the core. These insights felt like *downloads:* they came into his mind and heart with a clarity and urgency he could not ignore. And these insights felt deeply personal, because they helped him understand intense children's needs in the therapeutic process via his own direct experience as an intense child decades before. He saw that he had begun to have a new experience of the energy of exchange between children and the adults in their lives.

Howard trusted what he was being given. He began to incorporate this sense of knowing into his work with children and their families. The impact was dramatically positive. As he began to see these positive results in client after client, he continued to refine the methods he used to enhance that impact. Soon, he was receiving referrals to help the most challenging kids in and around his hometown of Tucson, Arizona. He was able to raise funds to open a counseling center, which he called the Center for the Difficult Child. Interns who learned his method found themselves more effective at helping challenging children than seasoned professionals using other methods. Word got out that he was able to cure ADHD. Other therapists began to clamor for Howard to teach them what he was doing.

Every time Howard saw a child learn to use her intensity well, he felt compelled to spread the word about his work. Still, at the time, the notion of sharing his approach with other therapists was terrifying. It seemed too different, too counter to what was generally being done. He feared being laughed out of the room. And he had never been someone who wanted to present to a bunch of strangers. Finally, he was pushed to give a presentation to colleagues in the area. As soon as he finished white-knuckling his way through it, he thought, "Never again!"

At the grocery store a few weeks later, Howard ran into a participant from the training he had given. To his astonishment, the participant overflowed with positive feedback about how the training had impacted and empowered him and his ten-person team. That was the point of take-off. Howard knew he had to move forward in sharing what he'd developed with as many other people as possible. He teamed up with Jennifer Easley to write his first book, *Transforming the Difficult Child*. Over 13 prior years, Jennifer – a brilliant therapist – had seen no impact on the families with whom she had worked. On the verge of quitting the field, Jennifer began to train with Howard, and seeing child after child turn around through this novel approach inspired her collaboration on this first Nurtured Heart book. That book has been in print since the early 2000s and continues to be a top-selling title on Amazon.

Writing about the approach and creating and conducting trainings for parents, caregivers, teachers, and treatment professionals became Howard's central focus. Since that time, tens of thousands of caring adults have learned the approach; it is being used in hundreds of classrooms across the U.S. and internationally; and it has been integrated into the clinical practices of thousands of therapists and other treatment professionals. Stories of transformation using the NHA now flood in from all over the world.

At age 9, Kalob was removed from his home along with his siblings due to his birth mother making and using methamphetamine. He lived in seven foster homes over three years before being reunited with one of his siblings and placed together with Mark and Sarah How in North Dakota. Sarah is a school psychologist, NHA Advanced Trainer, parent coach and children's author. Kalob say that he entered the How home "traumatized...I would ball up on the stairs and not talk, isolate myself, stay away from everybody." Kalob was given many labels, including severe PTSD, depression, ADHD and Reactive Attachment Disorder. The NHA, Sarah says, "gave us the 'how-to' in the trenches, first empowering and then equipping us to ferociously fight, as warriors, to reflect Kalob's greatness and re-define our relationships...Now, he is transparent, real, humorous, heartfelt and tearful about having gone from (his words) 'broken and alone' to 'normal."

PREPARING TO MAKE THE MOST OF THIS BOOK

Most people come to this approach because they need it. A child is spinning out of control; a teen is rebelling or withdrawing; a classroom or a school is saddled with more discipline problems than it can manage; a foster care system or a therapy office is failing to bring stability to challenged children or families.

Your Greatness Unfolding

People learning new approaches are sometimes asked to talk about the difficulties that brought them there and about the magnitude of the problems they have faced. We want to steer you in a different direction: dropping the story of what has gone wrong and using the pure energy of your emotions – perhaps including frustration, fear, and sadness – as fuel for the journey forward.

Truthfully, you have already used your frustration to make this next step of the journey. By coming to this book and this approach, you have placed the energy of your emotions around a challenging child into learning a new way. We applaud you using your frustration as fuel. We applaud your loving determination.

We are going to take you one step at a time through a process of understanding the Nurtured Heart Approach. We'll walk you through key stands and techniques. And we want you to know right now: you may feel resistant along the way.

You're going to bump into long-held beliefs about methods that may have worked with easier children but that have failed you with an intense child. Knowing this in advance, we're going to ask you to continue to take advantage of the beautiful energy of your frustration. Let it support you in taking the steps we recommend; in moving beyond your comfort zone and taking the risk inherent in trying new ways of relating to the children in your life.

Don't be thrown by your own resistance. Keep breathing. Use the frustration.

Let's begin.

Nurtured Heart Foundations

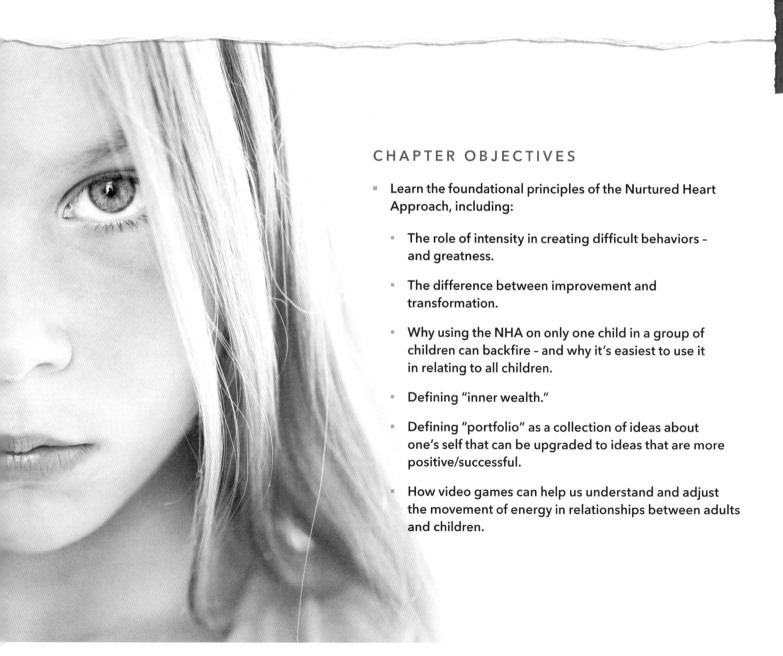

CHAPTER OBJECTIVES

- Learn the foundational principles of the Nurtured Heart Approach, including:

    - The role of intensity in creating difficult behaviors – and greatness.

    - The difference between improvement and transformation.

    - Why using the NHA on only one child in a group of children can backfire – and why it's easiest to use it in relating to all children.

    - Defining "inner wealth."

    - Defining "portfolio" as a collection of ideas about one's self that can be upgraded to ideas that are more positive/successful.

    - How video games can help us understand and adjust the movement of energy in relationships between adults and children.

In this chapter, we'll walk you through several foundational principles that underlie the techniques of the Nurtured Heart Approach.

We've taught these principles countless times in trainings. The responses we get from participants make each teaching a fresh and exhilarating experience.

As we dive in, the faces in the crowd are often pinched and stressed from the overwhelming task of dealing with the challenging child or children that motivated them to attend in the first place. The slide show proceeds; we explain these concepts, one at a time; and the expressions on participants' faces begin to shift dramatically. Foreheads relax. Corners of mouths turn up. Eyes widen with a combination of wonder and recognition. We hear a lot of variations on "Oh my goodness – that makes so much *sense!*" People begin to understand and recognize why the methods they've been using to try to help challenging children have been backfiring.

IMPROVEMENT VS. TRANSFORMATION

Psychiatric medications like Ritalin or Adderall are often used to try to temper or erase excess intensity. They will do that, but at a heavy price: suppression of the child's life force. While taking this tack is, in some cases, appealing for the sake of keeping the child and people around her safe – or, perhaps, for keeping the peace or one's sanity – it does not help the child learn to manage and direct the powerful force with which he or she has been gifted in this lifetime.

Medications may create some level of improvement – as measured by the child's ability to sit still, complete class work, or avoid getting into trouble – but they do not create transformation. Said more precisely: research into the impact of psychiatric medications for moderation of intensity does not demonstrate any long-term benefit. As soon as the medication is stopped, the child is back to square one. Before the meds take effect in the morning or wear off in the afternoon, the problems are still there, front and center. There has been no essential healing.

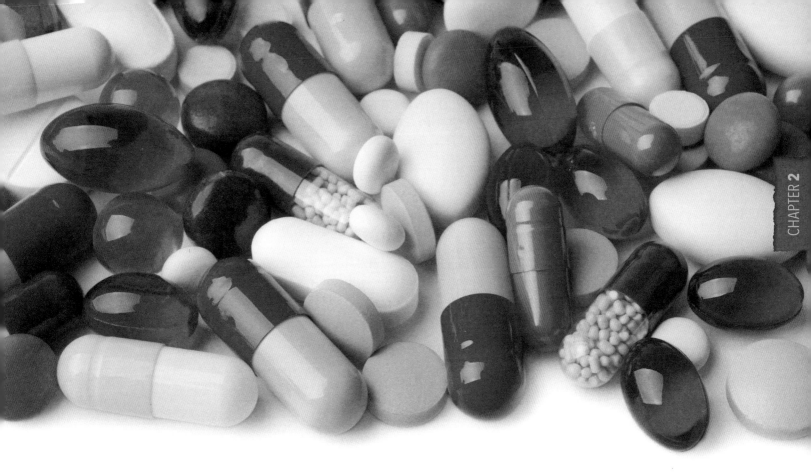

MEDICATIONS MAY CREATE SOME LEVEL OF IMPROVEMENT, BUT THEY DO NOT CREATE TRANSFORMATION.

If there were no way to transform a child's excess intensity into greatness, we might need to settle for improvement. Fortunately, there is a way to transformation that has been tested and proven for twenty-five years: the Nurtured Heart Approach.

WHAT IF...I HAVE ONE DIFFICULT CHILD AND OTHERS IN THE HOUSEHOLD WHO ARE NOT CHALLENGING? OR...I HAVE ONLY A COUPLE OF DIFFICULT STUDENTS IN MY CLASSROOM. SHOULD I USE THE APPROACH WITH THE CHALLENGING CHILDREN ONLY?

This approach works best when used with all children in a household. In the classroom, it is most beneficial when used on every student – not just the difficult students.

Focusing the NHA on rule-breakers only is likely to backfire in the following ways:

1. When the approach is used only on challenging children, the challenging child may continue with negative behaviors if they perceive that this is the only way to have continued access to Nurtured Heart connection. If a child ceases negative behavior and then "graduates" back to normal approaches that offer little to no rich connection in the absence of boundary-pushing, you'll probably end up right back where you started.

2. Marginal kids – those who aren't pushing boundaries, but who are considering it – may see the difficult kids getting the Nurtured Heart treatment and want some of that for themselves. They might begin to act out more in order to get it.

3. Well-behaved kids are likely to feel left out and annoyed, harboring a sense of inequity along with a sense that the teacher is not handling the challenges appropriately. It won't seem fair to them that the challenging children are getting so much more focus from adults. This is already an issue in many families and classrooms: the most difficult kid is the one that gets the most energy from adults. Using the approach with every child helps both well-behaved and challenging children to feel seen, heard, valued, meaningful and loved.

This approach was created specifically for challenging children, but is enriching and empowering for *all* children. It may need to be applied with greater intensity to more intense children, but it supports all children in growing their greatness.

INNER WEALTH

To use intensity well, kids need to be strong on the inside. From that strong place, they can learn to channel their intensity into greatness. The most challenging kid in the classroom becomes an amazing child with much to contribute. The child who couldn't behave herself for more than ten consecutive minutes becomes the child who shines most brightly, doing all that's asked of her and then some.

In Nurtured Heart parlance, we say that in order for this to happen, the child's *inner wealth* needs to be

built. Inner wealth is a belief in one's self that is developed through consistent, meaningful, direct experiences of success and value in relation to one's character and progressing sense of goodness and greatness. As is the case with any kind of wealth, the potential for expansion is endless. Inner wealth does not suggest egotism; it is simple knowledge that greatness is a given in self and others, and that every right choice (or avoidance of wrong choice) is an expression of that goodness and greatness.

INNER WEALTH IS A GROWING, PROGRESSING BELIEF IN ONE'S SELF THAT IS DEVELOPED AND EXPANDED THROUGH REPEATED DIRECT EXPERIENCES OF SUCCESS. INNER WEALTH IS AN UNFOLDING DISCOVERY OF WHO ONE REALLY IS AS A PERSON WHO IS MEANINGFUL, VALUED, AND HAS GREAT THINGS TO CONTRIBUTE. EVERY TIME A CHILD IS ON TRACK - EVEN IN SMALL WAYS - WE HAVE AN OPPORTUNITY TO BUILD INNER WEALTH BY ACKNOWLEDGING THE TRUTH OF THE GREATNESS WE SEE IN THOSE MOMENTS OF SUCCESS.

Endless inner wealth is available to every human being. There is no shortage of this resource—no one percent vs. 99 percent, as in the realm of economic wealth—and there is no competition around who has more. Each person's inner wealth adds to the riches of all, and everyone can be a billionaire.

Every time a child does something right – or even chooses *not* to do something *wrong* – we have an opportunity to build inner wealth by acknowledging that moment of success and the qualities of greatness it shows to already exist within the child. If the child's life were a movie, each of the thousands of frames shot each day would present an opportunity to create a growing sense of success through intentional verbal recognition and expressions of the appreciation we can come to feel. These recognitions come through the stands and techniques of the Nurtured Heart Approach.

CHANGING THE PORTFOLIO

Today, when you want to see samples of an artist's work, you go to the artist's Web site. Before the advent of digital imagery, visual artists would carry representative samples of their work in a big folder called a *portfolio*.

We like to say that each person has a portfolio of sorts that contains representative examples of who we think we are. An artist building her portfolio will choose images that represent her in her moments where she feels most worthy of celebration; a challenging child does this, too, when building her inner portfolio. She will fill it with moments where she has experienced the greatest energetic connection. A challenging child's portfolio might include images of his worst moments, because it was in those moments where she has felt most energetically celebrated!

Let's say that, at most, we've said "thank you" and "good job" when things have gone well; and that, in contrast, we have amped up communications that recognize poor choices. That child's highest-level poor choices can easily become the images that hang over the mantel as showcase moments of big connection. These images then wind up in his portfolio. He develops an upside-down idea of himself as bad, difficult, or wrong; as most meaningful, valued and worthy of connection from others when he is misbehaving. This becomes an unconscious "default setting" from which he lives his life. Most children develop this default in their very earliest years, before they learn to talk or walk.

Turning this around requires that those images be switched out for images of success and greatness. We don't throw away the entire portfolio; instead, over time, **we relentlessly support the child in re-framing the experience of who he really is.** We use every possible opportunity to point out success, embedding these reflections into first-hand experiences. Soon enough, the negative images he has been carrying around will be outweighed and outshined by greater positive images. The images of his less successful moments won't need to be thrown away, or even 'processed'; they will, rather, come to lose their negative traction and be seen in a new light.

In the film of *The Horse Whisperer*, Grace, a girl of about 13, has endured a terrible accident that killed her best friend and her best friend's horse and that injured her leg badly enough to require partial amputation. Grace's mother brings Grace and her traumatized horse to Tom, who is adept at re-training uncontrollable horses. In one scene, Grace is working in the stables and Tom comes in to ask her if she'd like to learn to drive the truck. She doesn't really want to – she doesn't think she can, because of her leg – but reluctantly agrees. Soon enough, she finds herself in the driver's seat, driving the car up the bumpy farm road with gentle coaxing from Tom in the passenger seat. He tips his hat forward and says he thinks he'll close his eyes for a few minutes, and that she should continue driving. "I can't," she protests, and he replies, "It's not a matter of whether you can or you can't. You *are*."

Nurtured Heart Action Step

Changing a child's portfolio means capturing her in moments like this one - where she incontrovertibly **is** doing something right. It means having the verve, perspective and words to let her know the beauty we see in her in those moments.

Through appreciative recognition, Tom challenged Grace with the truth of something she was already doing well. Try this: creatively find a half a dozen appreciative things you could say to 'confront' your child in the way Tom confronted Grace: where you can say, "it's not a question of whether you can or can't - you are!"

Make one or two such statements to the child. Notice your energy; notice the child's energy. "Sarah, the truth is that you have been very kind to your brother since he told you to leave him alone. You are being respectful and kind and I am so appreciative."

This next writing exercise is designed to help you see what's in your portfolio, and how it can be transformed through seeing what's right rather than focusing on mistakes or problems. This doesn't mean you are pretending to be perfect; it means you are putting your focus on what you do want instead of what you don't.

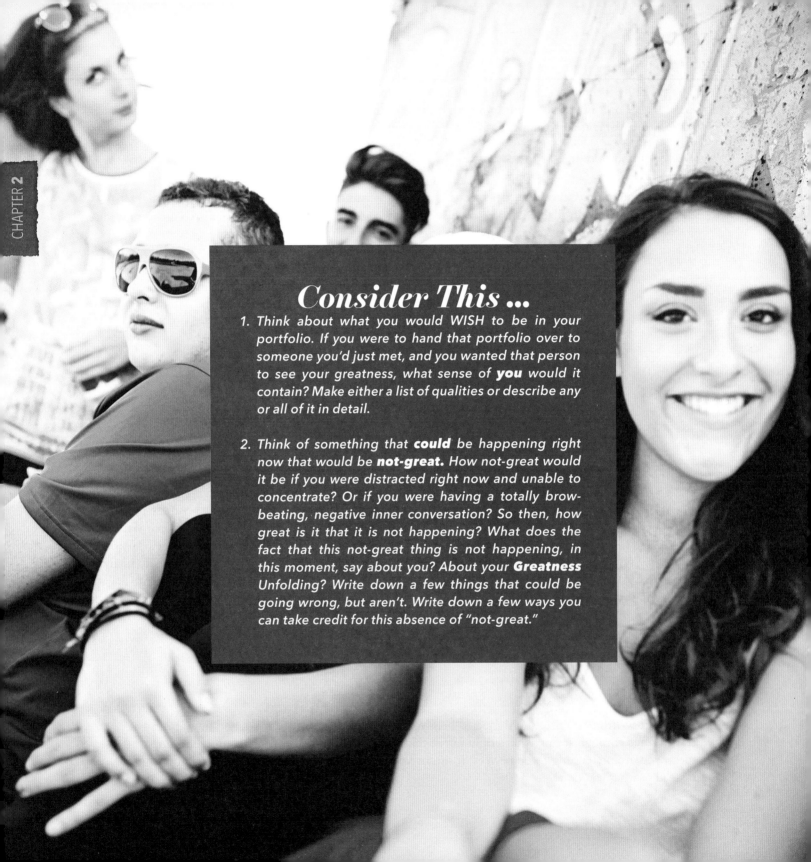

Consider This ...

1. *Think about what you would WISH to be in your portfolio. If you were to hand that portfolio over to someone you'd just met, and you wanted that person to see your greatness, what sense of **you** would it contain? Make either a list of qualities or describe any or all of it in detail.*

2. *Think of something that **could** be happening right now that would be **not-great.** How not-great would it be if you were distracted right now and unable to concentrate? Or if you were having a totally brow-beating, negative inner conversation? So then, how great is it that it is not happening? What does the fact that this not-great thing is not happening, in this moment, say about you? About your **Greatness** Unfolding? Write down a few things that could be going wrong, but aren't. Write down a few ways you can take credit for this absence of "not-great."*

Challenge

Begin to catch yourself and people around you in moments of success: where they are incontrovertibly successful, even to a small degree. You are creating these successes through purposeful awareness – by going way beyond the casual, passive mindset of "catching a child being good." Creating is a more powerful stance. You are doing it! *It's not a question of whether you can or can't, you are!*

TOYS R US

When you hand a child a new toy, what's the first thing he does? Read the instruction manual? Of course not! He starts to play. He tests out every button, function, and feature to see the full scope of its potential. When he tries a feature and it gives lots of feedback – flashing lights, maybe, or sounds, or interesting, engaging or funny movements – he's likely to return to it again and again if it fits his sense of what's compelling. If a feature fails to do anything interesting, he might go back once or twice to make sure it's a dud. Eventually, he'll declare it boring and not worth going back to.

If a feature gives a great response one time and then gives a lukewarm or zero response the next, the child is likely to continue to return to it. Will he get the big show? Or will nothing happen? That's great suspense – and as long as the show happens at least *some* of the time, he'll keep revisiting the feature.

Now think about this: *YOU as your child's favorite toy.* No other toy she'll ever have will approach its range of responses. It expresses the full spectrum of emotions. It's not just happy or sad, but rather your unique and ever-changing version of the gamut of human experiences, moods and emotions. It has an endless array of 'buttons' that elicit interesting reactions when pushed. One button might only get a mild reaction when Mom or Dad is having an okay day; on a day when moods are flaring, that same button might yield fireworks.

When things are going well, parents tend toward low-key responses and minimal energetic connection. What parent hasn't observed a child playing happily and tiptoed away, not wanting to disturb the positive moment or give the child any reason to act out? And then, when problems occur, adults lean way, way in. Kids get better 'broadband' from their favorite toys when they create problems. The toy is comparatively boring when things go well; its responses to negativity are far more energized and interesting - more bandwidth of connection and relationship.

CHILDREN CAN EASILY PERCEIVE THIS FACT – THAT THEY GET MORE INTENSELY AND INSTANTLY CONNECTED WITH THEIR FAVORITE TOYS (US!) WHEN THEY CREATE PROBLEMS. THE SAME TOY CAN BE PERCEIVED AS RELATIVELY BORING WHEN THINGS GO WELL.

An intense child craves strong connection and will be drawn to any toy's flashier, more surprising features. The intense child will most often choose those features that yield a more energized response. When the parent or the teacher is the toy in question, that child will be drawn inexorably toward those more interesting and energized responses – even if the situation also becomes unpleasant due to frustration, lecturing, or other reactions. Even a punitive response can feel like an incentive for the intense child, simply because it's MORE.

A less intense child may not go for that gold of the bigger, more energized response if she fears the consequences; for the more intense child, warnings and conventional consequences only add fuel to the fire. It's all energy, and the more energy, the better – at least for an intense child. The intense child perceives more energy as greater connection and meaning.

Children read energy like Braille. They read into their reality at the level of energy; this is, essentially, how they put two and two together in translating the meaning of their lives. Energy is what they respond to; it's what teaches them how to be in the world.

If we want children to follow rules and adhere to what we consider 'good behavior,' and we give them so much more of ourselves – of our energy – when they misbehave, we have the dynamic upside down. This upside-down energy means that the child feels more loved, valued and celebrated in relation to problems. Upside-down energy is a clear statement that the way to get connected fast is to dive into some form of negativity: misbehavior, opposition, complaining, sadness, depression, anxiety.

This upside-down energy is the rule rather than the exception in most modern cultures. It's everywhere around us – even in situations where there is surface positivity. Remember the last time you had a 'charged' response with a child because of a poor choice you thought that child had made. How great is the charge of your response when the child is *not* making a poor choice?

THE INTENSE CHILD PERCEIVES MORE ENERGY AS GREATER CONNECTION AND MEANING.

The Nurtured Heart Approach is more about relationship than attention. The energetic exchange that occurs around the child's positive behaviors is a channel that runs in both directions, with inputs from both the child and the adult. It's not a one-way energy, where an adult "gives more attention" – it is a circuit that strengthens and expands with repeated traverses as the child moves further in a positive direction. As adults, we are not merely attuning or offering attention; we are *building relationship* that is founded in positivity.

> # Consider This ...
>
> **SET AN INTENTION, FOR A DAY, TO NOTICE THE WAYS THE CHILDREN IN YOUR LIFE PERCEIVE YOUR ENERGIES OF RELATIONSHIP. WHERE DO YOU RADIATE THE MOST ENERGY? HOW DO CHILDREN RESPOND?**

Shifting this upside-down energy requires that we learn to refuse to give *ourselves* in response to negative behaviors. Normal, traditional ways of responding to problems have us trying to teach lessons in the midst of the issue. When we offer up the most intense relationship to children at those times when things are going wrong, we energetically tell them, "Don't do that!" while in effect handing them a $100 bill. We accidentally give the gift of ourselves in juicy, energized forms of relationship when things are going wrong. We need to hand out those energetic $100 bills in response to what's going well.

If we do this consistently, the children in our lives begin to see that they don't need to misbehave to get us to acknowledge and connect with them. Children need to experience us seeing them profoundly *when things aren't going wrong*. That's the perfect time to launch energized responses and to convey the beauty we see in them. *That's when the lessons truly land.*

CHILDREN NEED TO EXPERIENCE US SEEING THEM PROFOUNDLY WHEN THINGS AREN'T GOING WRONG.

On a day when Howard gave an in-service at an elementary school, he showed up early and began to set up in the library. A group of kids worked quietly on an assignment nearby.

One child began to get distracted. The librarian was right there with him in an instant, talking to him softly and encouraging him to stay focused and not make noise. She was kind, respectful, and loving. The child quieted down for a moment, but the moment didn't last long. Soon, he was disrupting the group again, and several others were following suit.

You may have noticed this dynamic in a classroom before, and figured that this is just the way things go when kids are all together. Kids don't want to sit still, be quiet and do classwork, right? They disrupt because they have trouble controlling themselves, and they need redirection or correction when their impulses overwhelm their desire to follow the rules. Consider, though, that other energetics may be at play; that the teacher, as her students' 'favorite toy,' could choose to interact with them in a way that makes following the rules and doing classwork more appealing than breaking rules and goofing off.

What message did the librarian inadvertently send to the prospective troublemaker? "If you want a kind and loving adult to come over and spend time with you, break a rule." And what happened as soon as the child settled down? She walked away. Adults might let hours of neutral or even good behavior go unacknowledged, but as soon as a child starts to push the boundaries, they're on it at lightning speed – as though someone had caught them on a hook and reeled them in.

No matter how busy we are, no matter how overwhelmed, most everyone can drop everything in response to a problem, just as that caring teacher did in the library that day. *The reality is that we are never too busy for a problem.* Other children pick up on this same message: that acting out is the fastest and most assured route to intense connection with an adult. Additional children are likely to follow suit as they recognize that this is the game in play.

The librarian's response is in perfect alignment with the average 'positive' approach. Consider the energetic undercurrent being created. To *get* the adult in the room, all you need to do is break a rule. Whether the adult in question yells and lectures or sweetly redirects, he or she is still showing up for negativity. These methods are well intentioned, but they keep the metaphoric $100 bills for negativity flowing.

Loving, caring school counselors and administrators are often inundated with acting-out children who are referred their way for much the same reason. It doesn't take an intense child long to figure out that he or she can get a great version of kind, loving relationship by getting kicked out of class over and over again. It's a setup; fortunately, it's a setup that can be shifted quite easily.

We don't want anyone to stop being kind and loving. What we are proposing is an adjustment in timing that allows the child to experience a congruent version of success, where doing good or not breaking rules consistently brings the connection they seek. When the timing is right, the adult can ride the resultant wave of energy, accomplishing a great deal of accelerated character building through simple, powerful recognitions and appreciations.

To convey to the child that energy for negativity is no longer available, we take the first Stand of the Nurtured Heart Approach: Absolutely No!: I refuse to give energy to negativity.

Much more will be said about this Stand in chapters to come.

ADULTS MIGHT LET HOURS OF NEUTRAL OR EVEN GOOD BEHAVIORS GO UNACKNOWLEDGED, BUT AS SOON AS A CHILD STARTS TO PUSH THE BOUNDARIES, THEY'RE ON IT AT LIGHTNING SPEED.

NOT ABOUT IGNORING PROBLEM BEHAVIORS

A question that pops up early on in a room full of parents learning this approach is: "Am I supposed to just ignore it when my child behaves badly?" No. We will be recommending complete accountability when lines are crossed.

Ignoring invites the child to 'up the ante' – to escalate the questionable behavior in an effort to elicit a response. If you've tried the "ignore it" tack, you may have seen it work, at least some of the time, with less intense children…and fuel the fire beyond belief in more intense children. Ignoring will inspire the intense child to get more creative in his efforts to rope you into energizing negative choices.

Upholding the First Stand is about an active refusal to energize the behaviors you want to minimize. *Active refusal* is not ignoring. It is about intentionally, consistently pausing the energy flow between you and your child when a rule is broken, while attentively waiting for the first opportunity to energize the child when problems are not happening. In that moment where no rule is being broken, it's time to give the gift of yourself wholeheartedly in response to all that is going right.

The video games most kids love are a good example of the ways we can de-energize our responses to the negative (Stand One), pour more energy into what's going well (Stand Two), and always give a consequence for a broken rule (Stand Three).

VIDEO GAME THEORY

Most parents know kids who cannot focus on homework for more than a couple of minutes at a time, but can play a video game for hours with mastery and accomplishment. This becomes far less paradoxical and mysterious when we consider the way the energetics of these games are built. The energy in the video game is right side up.

In video games, the incentives are strong and predictable. They confront a child with success - points are scored, sounds and visuals provide energized recognition. Video games also always deliver a consequence every time a rule is broken, even fractionally, and it does so seamlessly in the moment. The child is back in the game quickly, more inspired than ever to not break the rules again.

In the world of gaming, the timing of incentives and consequences is always right and the energetic payoffs are always right side up. With this kind of structure, kids can "play life" with the same zeal and sense of accomplishment they experience while immersed in a video game. This structure helps them thrive and flourish. The structure is all-encompassing; everything within that structure is clear and predictable.

THE THREE STANDS: AN INTRODUCTION

Think of these Stands as commitments and as a set of firm guidelines. They are meant to support you in building the resolve and clarity needed to have powerful impact.

You'll consider these often as you learn the Approach and begin to feel out what is in alignment with the NHA and what isn't. The Stands will also provide a point of reference to which you can return when you feel you've inadvertently veered off track. They serve as a kind of GPS, helping you seamlessly detect when you are off course and to recalculate your route to success.

THE FIRST STAND

ABSOLUTELY NO!: I refuse to energize negativity.

With this stand, you refuse to reward or respond to negativity with energy, connection or relationship – to give energetic $100 bills for negativity. This stand is a clear refusal to give the gift of *you* when things are going awry. It's a commitment to undo the child's perception that he or she receives the juiciest relationship (the energies of words, emotions and actions, coupled with the degree of connection) from adults when things are going wrong.

Again, this is *not* about ignoring bad behavior, but about refusing to give energy to negativity. ***Positivity doesn't work* until we build the foundation that we are no longer available in response to negativity.**

This stand is the one that makes Nurtured Heart different from other seemingly 'positive' parenting methods. It is the step that sets the whole energetic conversion in motion.

THE SECOND STAND

ABSOLUTELY YES!: I relentlessly create and energize positivity and success. I energize and nurture firsthand experiences of success; in fact, I refuse *not* to.

You will learn to deliver clear, powerful appreciations strong enough to navigate around a child's defenses. In learning the techniques and relentlessly employing them to give evidence of greatness, you'll ensure that recognition and acknowledgment are felt and digested as success. This Stand is about doing everything you can to see the greatness in the child and communicating that greatness often and with intention. It goes beyond ordinary levels of positivity to recognitions that honor underlying character. It gives tools for describing, to the child, how his character is reflected in his everyday choices and actions, using heart-level language that hits home with even the most resistant child.

THE THIRD STAND

ABSOLUTELY CLEAR! I maintain clear rules and always give a brief, un-energized consequence when a rule is broken.

Not giving energy to negativity doesn't work by itself; one must show that relationship *is* fully available through appreciation, recognition and acknowledgment (positivity). These form a foundation where clarity can be achieved though clear rules and clear, un-energized consequences.

JUST SAY NO: FOCUS ON THE FIRST STAND

Although this is a strongly positive approach, the first stand is all about creating the vital foundation of saying "No!" which, in this context, is about letting the children in our care know that we are no longer available through negativity. We feel that this stand is most important of all in setting the stage for true transformation.

As you read on, you'll see how the "No!" of the approach is anchored by the second stand of relentless, creative positive acknowledgement and the third stand of clarity, where the resultant consequence—a simple reset—leads us back to an ever-greater "Yes!"

The First Stand
ABSOLUTELY NO!: *REFUSAL TO ENERGIZE NEGATIVITY*

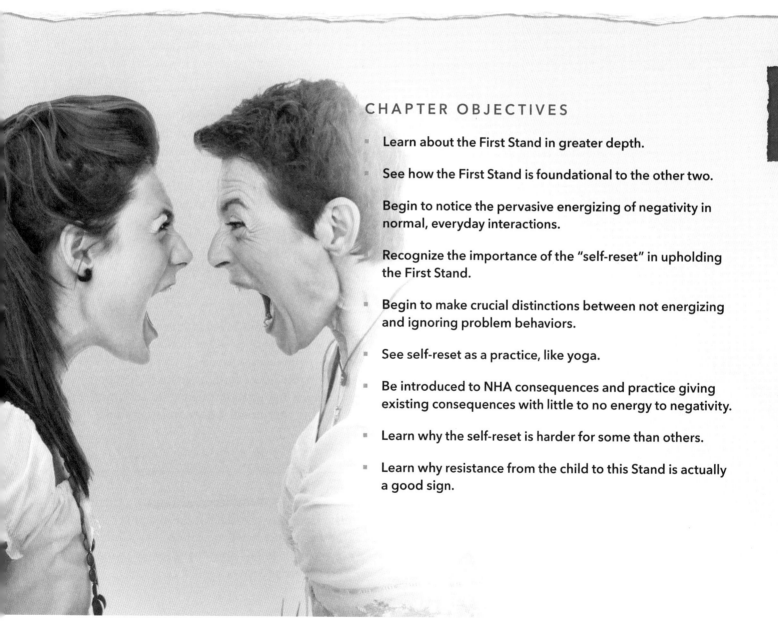

CHAPTER OBJECTIVES

- Learn about the First Stand in greater depth.

- See how the First Stand is foundational to the other two.

- Begin to notice the pervasive energizing of negativity in normal, everyday interactions.

- Recognize the importance of the "self-reset" in upholding the First Stand.

- Begin to make crucial distinctions between not energizing and ignoring problem behaviors.

- See self-reset as a practice, like yoga.

- Be introduced to NHA consequences and practice giving existing consequences with little to no energy to negativity.

- Learn why the self-reset is harder for some than others.

- Learn why resistance from the child to this Stand is actually a good sign.

Co-author Melissa was in an airport waiting to board a flight. A parent stood in front of her, holding the hand of her preschool-aged child. While the child stood calmly, Mom focused on other things. When the child started to whine, squirm, and drag on her mother's arm, the mother's attention turned fully to the child.

"Stop that!" she snapped. "Stand still. Quit whining. We have a long flight ahead of us!"

The child stopped briefly, and the mom turned away again as soon as the child stopped breaking the rule. More squirming and whining followed. This time, it was louder, and Mom's temper flared more. Others in line for the flight looked at each other and shook their heads, knowing that if the child didn't fall asleep on the flight, they might all be in for a noisy journey.

Many of us have been that parent, waiting in line for the flight where others throw us dirty looks for not being able to keep a child in our care quiet and calm. Parents can come to feel as though they have no control. They use the methods they've learned, which – even in the case of the most positive parenting methods – tend to fuel the exact fires they are trying to put out. The more intense the acting-out, the more intensely they apply these traditional methods, and the worse the situation tends to get. As the child perceives connection and relationship in context of negativity, even innocent attempts to set reasonable limits become gas for the fire.

Consider This...

As you move through your day, notice the way in which the negative tends to be energized in interactions all around you. Begin to notice how your own soul feels called to respond to problems, mistakes, and rule breaking. Notice how these responses – whether in the form of gentle redirections, lectures, pep talks, warnings, angry outburst, or attempts to set limits – impact cooperation, compliance and the general tenor of relationships.

Less intense children will likely respond to reprimands, angry comments, lectures, threats, or redirection by stopping the unwanted behavior. Children with greater intensity are likely to keep acting out, caught between the fear of unwanted consequences and the need for intense energetic connection. Children with more than their share of intensity are more likely to form energetic impressions that they get so much more juicy and connected relationship – better broadband – through negativity.

The First Stand is the first step to shifting this dynamic:

Absolutely No!

I REFUSE TO ENERGIZE NEGATIVITY.

I WILL NOT REWARD NEGATIVITY WITH MY ENERGY, CONNECTION, OR RELATIONSHIP.

Following this Stand is about choosing the quality and quantity of the energies we radiate: about 'saving our souls' for what we *do* want. This begins with refusing to be a more exciting "toy" when things are going wrong.

STAND ONE IS ABOUT SAVING OUR SOULS FOR WHAT WE DO WANT INSTEAD OF GIVING OURSELVES ABUNDANTLY TO WHAT WE DON'T WANT.

KEY TO SUCCESS WITH THE FIRST STAND: THE SELF-RESET

In Stand Three, you will learn how to reset a child who is breaking a rule. This is the all-purpose Nurtured Heart consequence. It's powerful, but in truth, it isn't really even a consequence – it's a momentary and purposeful pause in connection with a built-in chance to make a different choice. Ideally, the reset will carry only a fraction of the intensity the adult brings to responses to positive behaviors.[2]

However this strikes you, put it in the hopper for later. It will make far more sense when you reach that point in this workbook. The reason we bring it to your attention now is because there are really two forms of the reset:

1. The one given to the child in response to a broken rule; and,

2. The *self-reset*, which you give yourself when you're tempted to energize negativity (to not adhere to the First Stand).

You will learn and practice the self-reset before learning to reset others. Almost everyone who learns and uses this approach comes to treat the self-reset as an ongoing practice. Ideally, this self-reset just happens as a consequence of refusing to energize negativity and stepping into positivity, and of giving a simple, un-energized consequence when rules are broken. These Stands cannot be upheld in a congruent way (with the external expression matching the internal state) if we are not resetting within ourselves as well, and resetting does just happen of its own accord when we hold to the Approach's Stands; however, an awareness of the need to reset one's self, and direct work on this as a skill, leads to a more steadfast vantage point and more empowered impact.

Seeing tiny increments of what's wrong with the picture is in our collective DNA. We wouldn't be here unless our ancestors were great at detecting the beginnings of a dangerous situation. Our modern-day version of this ancient instinct is a constant

---

[2] While major infractions may call for some restoration, the majority of rule-breaking behaviors respond beautifully to a simple reset once the approach is in motion.

scanning for even the smallest of problems and reacting to them without much discernment. We're not so good at doing the transverse, although on any given day, *so much more is going right than is going wrong.* It's more a default setting than a purposeful, intentional use of our energy. Energizing negativity is a habit, and it can be shifted. That shift becomes an ongoing practice: a kind of relationship yoga.

ON ANY GIVEN DAY, MUCH MORE IS GOING RIGHT THAN GOING WRONG.

THE YOGA OF RESETTING YOURSELF

A yoga practice involves a foundational aspect of maintaining focus on the breath. Any yoga practitioner knows that this focus slips and is restored many times during each practice session. Minds wander. Old patterning re-emerges. We remember: *oh, yeah, the breath.* And we're back, until the next distraction. Over weeks, months, and years of practice, this re-focusing becomes more automatic and less of it is required.

The self-reset is the same. The more you practice, the more it becomes automatic. Instead of going a thousand miles down a road of negativity, you only go five hundred. You remember your intention sooner. You return to the First Stand. *Reset.* Then, after more practice, you knock it down to about twenty-five miles.

Any expectation that you'll never go into negativity means expecting yourself to not be human and not make mistakes. Even masters of this approach sometimes accidentally energize negativity in ways both subtle and profound. An enormous part of the personal process of learning and applying the NHA is catching ourselves in those moments and resetting.

Ultimately, the self-reset is one of the greatest gifts we can give – to our children and to ourselves. It's a fast track to resilience, that quality that enables us to persevere and triumph over adversity.

THE SELF-RESET IS A FAST TRACK TO RESILIENCE, THAT QUALITY THAT ENABLES US TO PERSEVERE AND TRIUMPH OVER ADVERSITY.

In learning to reset ourselves, we live the truth that mistakes happen, and that each next moment is an opportunity for renewal. Each new moment holds a fresh start. Our mission, should we choose to accept it, is to re-focus on greatness in that new moment: to turn away when the siren song of negativity calls to us, and to become adept at using the energy of what has frustrated us to renew to next levels of greatness in the moments that follow.

The self-reset is what enables adults to resist going down the road of negativity or to circle back if we have already made strides in that direction; and to then show up fully, with total, juicy presence, for the child when things are going well.

GETTING STARTED WITH THE FIRST STAND

Begin to play with this notion of steadfast refusal to energize negativity. As you notice your urge to scold, lecture, or otherwise react strongly to your child's negative behavior, tell yourself, "Reset!" and drain as much energy out of your response as possible. Keep in mind that even the kindest intention to mediate or lovingly intervene in a negative situation is a form of giving yourself to negativity and is cause to choose to reset to the first stand.

Find something in the situation to appreciate. Comment on it as soon as it feels doable for you. Waiting until the moment when the rule that was broken is *not* being broken is the key. Give the same lecture that wanted to emerge in the midst of negativity, but give it during the moments where those rules are being followed. Explore positive, authentic statements that can be shared in those moments, and notice the much stronger impact of this kind of 'lecture.' "Sarah, the great attitude you're showing now will get you far in life. Being kind to others, as you are now, is a warm and welcoming way to be helpful in tense situations…and you are doing it!"

Recognize that any time the child is *not* doing something wrong, success can be recognized in some way. The next chapter will go into great detail on this point.

The more intense the child, the more intense the application and determination required to convert upside-down energy to energy that is congruent, useful and purposeful. This isn't *always* the case – sometimes, an intense child dives into this new mode of positivity without so much as a glance backward, as though he's been waiting his whole life for you to figure this out – but it usually is. Daily commitment to practicing the approach, starting with the first stand, is key; so is "meeting" the intensity of the child by refusing to energize his negative choices with any evidence of our own energized reactivity.

Challenge

1. Write a list of the usual consequences you give your child for breaking rules. For each consequence, make a few notes about how you will enact them with as little engaged energy as possible. If you have a co-parent, discuss this with him or her and do some role-playing for practice. Make it your mission to keep consequences as simple and un-energized as possible until it is time to learn Stand Three and the full reset.

2. Try writing out or role-playing some after-the-fact energizing statements you might use with a child. For example: "Thank you for not screaming at your brother right now. That helps all of us feel more peaceful and happy to be together. You're making a respectful choice right now."

HOW SHOULD CONSEQUENCES BE GIVEN?

In Chapter Six, you will learn to give consequences in a way that won't reward negativity. Until then, use the same consequences you've used in the past when rules are broken, but deliver them with as little verve and intensity as possible. At those times, avoid energized exchanges, lectures, sermons, and warnings, as these feed the very fires of negativity you're trying to put out. Keep consequences concise and low-energy with as few words and emotions as possible. Once they are over, watch for any opportunity to acknowledge what the child is doing right and what is going well. Express your appreciation as fully as you can.

Consider This...

Modern brain research demonstrates that thoughts of gratitude boost dopamine, the same neurotransmitter boosted by the antidepressant Wellbutrin. Dopamine is a key neurotransmitter in the stimulation of both interest and reward. Pleasurable experiences like eating good food, having positive physical intimacy, or playing a video game all amp up dopamine activity in our bodies. When we are grateful toward others, specific circuits are impacted that increase the pleasure we feel with social interactions.

*The Nurtured Heart Approach is a gratitude practice. It goes beyond standard versions of these practices ("Something I am grateful for is..."). It is an active seeking-out of reasons for gratitude - reasons both large and small - and it rides the waves of gratitude to build character and greatness so children become **great**-filled.*

The NHA gives us tools for locating and reveling in what we are grateful for, even on a day where a lot has gone wrong. It expands creativity in finding things to be grateful for: that we managed to get ourselves showered and off to work on a morning where all we wanted to do was stay in bed; or that our child did not break the rule about arguing, although she was obviously tempted. In using the NHA, we open door after door to ever-expanding realms of greatness and great-full-ness that are not only sustainable on their own, but that can produce additional manifestations that we can see and acknowledge. The sky is truly the limit.

If you feel you must impart a lesson of some kind to the child in the wake of wrongdoing, make it your mission to teach it only in this alternative way. Do so in a context of acknowledging a related success once the consequence is complete.

Challenge

As you begin to withhold energy for negativity, notice how your child responds. Write about your experience or talk about it with your partner or a trusted friend.

BE PREPARED...

As the child is faced with this new dynamic, expect some pushback. This dance of energy for negativity is the one she knows best, and she is probably not going to let go of it without a fight. Think of an example in your own life of a pattern that didn't serve you, but that you maintained just because it felt familiar. Maybe you had a job that felt wrong to you, but you stayed because it was comfortable in some important ways. Maybe you had a habit that was destructive to your health, but choosing to kick it felt like too much uncertainty to bear.

The truth is: no matter how big the negativity you're facing, you're always going to reset yourself, anyway, *no matter what*. You're simply *never not* going to come back to yourself. It might take years or a lifetime, but it's going to happen. You can hold on to worry, misery, or doubt (WMDs) until your last days on earth, or until next year, but why not see if you can access that return to greatness sooner? Maybe immediately. It's never *not* a choice.

Your Greatness Unfolding...

You already have a profound ability to reset yourself. You do it all the time. If you didn't, the challenges of your life would have derailed you by now. But here you are, reading this book, learning, and holding a deep and profound intention to foster greatness in children. You might not have realized that you were resetting to get yourself back on track. Now, you can be more conscious about using that energy in a truly intentional way.

You have always collaborated with your own intensity to mobilize and energize your next steps in growth. This method is your ally in making that collaboration more mindful, in service of the life you want to live and the relationships you want to have.

NO BLAME!

By now, we hope you recognize that even the best-intentioned parent, educator, or treatment professional might be unable to enact transformation for a challenging child using the normal, traditional methods previously at his or her disposal. And we hope you can see that the child is also not to blame when traditional methods fail. The parent, teacher or child is not the problem; the problem has been the methods at their disposal. If you've been holding any kind of self-blame or blame of another around a difficult child's choices, you can let that go.

With a method that is energetically aligned, everything changes. In the next chapter, we'll help you set a few intentions that will continue to move you in the direction of that energetic alignment.

Nurtured Heart Intentions
IN SUPPORT OF THE SECOND STAND

CHAPTER OBJECTIVES

- Introduction to several intentions that support the Second Stand of the NHA ("Absolutely YES!"):

  - Making success inevitable by seeing success in "baby steps."

  - Choosing how we see things via the Toll Taker intention.

  - Learning to make miracles from molecules instead of mountains from molehills.

- Distinguishing non-specific, vague praise from relationship-building, inner wealth-building Nurtured Heart recognitions.

- See the value of "setting the bar for success" as a vital step along the way.

- Learning to "break it down and add it up" and "pixelate."

- Learning why, despite what you might initially think, you DO have time to give positive acknowledgements to your child.

- Learning why those who say too much praise is a problem are wrong – and why.

- Understanding the balance of "time-in" with time-out.

The Second Stand is about creating first-hand experiences of success. As we actively support the child in building inner wealth and a positive portfolio, the child begins to recognize that negativity is no longer the best way to create intense connection and relationship. Energy for negativity is no longer available. As relationship is abundantly offered around positive choices that highlight the beauty of qualities of character already at play, the child is drawn to live out ever-greater levels of greatness. Stand Two gives adults tools to fill the space created by Stand One, the refusal to energize negativity:

> ## *Absolutely Yes!*
>
> **I RELENTLESSLY CREATE AND ENERGIZE POSITIVITY AND SUCCESS.**
>
> **I ENERGIZE AND NURTURE FIRST-HAND EXPERIENCES OF SUCCESS.**
>
> **I REFUSE NOT TO. I REFUSE TO FORGET.**

In this Stand, we balance commitment to refuse to energize negativity with an intention to give ourselves – our vital energy, our relationship and connection, our "bells and whistles" – to what we *do* want. In the past, we most likely have rung those bells and blown those whistles in response to choices that have riled or incensed us. We've already had plenty of practice making noise in response to behaviors! This Stand is about a choice to do so in response to what's going right as well as what's *not* going wrong.

If you're parenting a difficult child, you might think it close to impossible to capture that child in experiences of success. We understand, because in the culture in which most of us grew up, the bar has typically been held high in terms of achievement. However, as the child's smallest successes are acknowledged and success becomes impossible to avoid, your child will accrue the inner wealth needed to meet the highest expectations and challenges.

BABY STEPS

Imagine a baby getting ready to take her first steps: holding on to something, making adorable baby sounds, letting go and taking one step, and then another! Then: Plop! Down she goes. What do you say? "Your form could have been better!" Probably not. "Two steps? You should have taken ten." Of course we wouldn't say that!

"Oh my goodness! You did it!" is more likely to spring from your lips. "You took your first steps! How wonderful!" Your appreciative and admiring words would hold the vivid flashes of excitement that you radiate from head to toe. Any expression that comes through us in the moment of connecting with that baby comes straight from the heart.

We celebrate every increment of that baby's progress toward walking. We wouldn't think to be critical. Indeed, we're likely to seed the steps before they even begin. We might admire how the baby exercises her legs and arms as a prelude to pulling herself off of the ground. Even if that baby were developmentally different, the adults charged with her care would find ways to encourage her movement toward greater functionality and independence.

Unfortunately, we tend to lose that instinct for responsive delight as children leave babyhood. Before we know it, we're sitting that same child down and giving her a lecture about how her behavior, grades or life choices could stand improvement.

To internalize this intention of the Nurtured Heart Approach, hold in your awareness the image of that baby taking its first steps. Try to recall how that baby can do no wrong: no strict expectations, just joy and awe in the moment; no bar held high, just an attentive, heart-open state where every increment in the right direction is something to recognize, appreciate, acknowledge and celebrate. Feel yourself wanting to applaud even the efforts that barely get off the ground.

*THAT BABY TAKING ITS FIRST STEPS CAN DO NO WRONG: NO STRICT EXPECTATIONS, JUST AN ATTENTIVE, HEART-OPEN STATE WHERE EVERY INCREMENT IN THE RIGHT DIRECTION IS SOMETHING TO RECOGNIZE, APPRECIATE, ACKNOWLEDGE AND CELEBRATE. **FEEL YOURSELF WANTING TO APPLAUD EVEN THE EFFORTS THAT BARELY GET OFF THE GROUND.***

Whether we excitedly acknowledge her every movement toward walking or critique her shortcomings, this baby will toddle, trip, fall, and clamber to her feet again. Eventually, she'll move from wobbly walk to confident stride to swift run. Even if we try to stop her, success is inevitable, barring a disability that impacts this process. It's the baby's nature to be great. Every movement and evolution is an expression of that greatness, completely unfettered by ego or fear.

When I tell parents that the Nurtured Heart Approach involves noticing and acknowledging the child moving in the direction of success as well as appreciating what *isn't* going wrong, they at first cannot always envision themselves able to find successes to acknowledge. But if they can remember those first steps, and then the often-untapped realm of exploration on the way to those steps, that exploration itself comes to inspire them. They begin to feel into the notion that success is not an un-scalable mountain or a bar held too high, but rather a mindset of acknowledging and recognizing success that already exists.

This is true of the sprout that reveals itself well before any expectation of harvest, and it is true of every human being – even the most difficult child. As we acknowledge the beauty of that first inkling of movement in the desired direction, *we become a vital part of creating successes that might not otherwise exist.* We are harvesting a vision of things to come.

This intention will reveal to you how to create successes that would not otherwise exist. You will develop an ability to find ways to see and acknowledge choices that would have most likely escaped most traditional lenses of success.

Challenge

BEGIN TO SEE THE BABY STEPS HAPPENING ALL AROUND YOU. LOOK WITH FRESH EYES AT EVERYTHING YOU AND OTHERS DO IN YOUR DAILY LIFE. RECOGNIZE THAT SIMPLY SEEING AND NOTICING IS, IN ITSELF, AN ACT OF APPRECIATION. MAKE IT YOUR BUSINESS TO TAKE SOME OF THESE APPRECIATIVE MOMENTS OF NOTICING AND PUT THEM INTO WORDS OF ACKNOWLEDGMENT.

THIS IS WAY BEYOND "CATCHING A CHILD BEING GOOD"—WE ARE RENEWING TO AN EMPOWERED MODE OF "CREATING A CHILD BEING GREAT."

CHAPTER 4

THE DANCING TOLL TAKER

One bright morning, a man drives across the San Francisco Bay Bridge. He comes to the line of tollbooths and notices a toll taker who is behaving quite differently from the others. The toll taker is dancing up a storm in his small cubicle. Curious, the man moves into that toll taker's lane and pulls up to the window. Upbeat music plays from a boom box inside the booth.

"Good morning!" the man says. "You look like you're having a great time in there."

"Yes!" the toll taker says. "I have the best job in the world. I have this incredible view. I just got to see the sun rise, and other days, I get to watch it set. Besides that, I'm listening to my favorite tunes and I'm studying to be a professional dancer, and I can practice while I'm being paid!"

The man looks around at the other toll takers. "Well, the others don't look nearly as happy as you do."

"Oh, those guys in the stand-up coffins?" replies the dancing toll taker. "They're no fun."

You get to interpret your reality any way you like. You can be the guy in the stand-up coffin, dreading days full of traffic noise, exhaust and drudgery; or you can be the dancing toll taker, creating joy for yourself wherever you happen to be.

So, you see: we get to *choose* how we see things, just like the dancing toll taker. Moment by moment, we can choose to see unfolding beauty. Contrary to what some might seem to believe, we are not held captive by any other way of seeing the world.

This is beyond conventional notions about whether the cup is half-empty or half-full. Even if the glass is completely empty, we can choose to imagine what was or could be in there. We are only limited by the glory of our imaginations and our ability to detect the slivers of success that are always there for the taking.

Why not perceive that success is the primary possibility; offer energized gratitude for that success; and let the energy of that greatness and momentum feed your the next levels of success? It's always your choice, after all. In fact, it's never NOT your choice. You are the director and producer of the movie that is your life.

YOU GET TO CHOOSE HOW YOU SEE THINGS;
YOU ARE THE DIRECTOR AND PRODUCER OF
THE MOVIE THAT IS YOUR LIFE.

MIRACLES FROM MOLECULES

Most of us have powerfully developed the skill of making mountains out of molehills, even if those gears are rarely engaged. We've all encountered people who are masters of squeezing every ounce of potential negativity out of what is wrong. Some have elevated this practice to a virtual art form.

This ability is part of our evolutionary heritage. Being able to detect even the slightest hint of danger – and to extrapolate how that small hint might turn into something life threatening – helped our ancestors survive long enough to pass on their DNA. If they hadn't been good at seeing what was wrong with the picture, we wouldn't be here now.

Today, this kind of vigilance is more a liability than an advantage – at least for those of us fortunate enough to live in places where our basic needs for safety and nourishment are met. An incident at work, some energized words with a friend (even if it's part of an overall great time together), having a near-miss at an intersection (even if no accident occurred where there could have been one), worries about money or school (even when, overall, everything is actually going all right and could be worse), regrets about past mistakes and concerns about future problems (even though here we are, wonderful, just as we are): all of these are par for the course for most of us.

Without an intention to focus on successes instead of problems, we are prone to default to being lured into negativity. The smallest bit of anything that is or could be wrong can grab us by the shirttails and take us for a spin that lasts hours, weeks, months, or years.

Fortunately, just as we can change the default settings of our computers, we can change default settings within ourselves. We can go to the mat of positivity with the same relentless mindset.

Most of us have the skills required to inflate even minor versions of everyday problems, allowing them to take up most of our awareness for hours, days, or weeks. We do the same with problems and issues related to our children's behavior. Our culture sanctions this: see problem, dwell on problem, attack problem, solve problem. We have the verbiage to wax poetic about what is wrong, but for most of us, the language of what's right falls short.

Consider what would happen if we dedicated our resources to finding successes to acknowledge and celebrate.

How would life feel if, instead of making mountains out of molehills, we applied our considerable talent and energies to finding successes, goodness, and greatness that already exist in the moment? *What if we made miracles out of molecules?*

What if we had language and vision to support expression of the appreciation we have for what we've wanted all along – for the gratitude we feel when problems *aren't happening?* What if we became adept at telling children about how beautiful it is when they are not arguing, fussing, or fighting? About how great their choices are when they are not procrastinating or refusing to do what is needed?

A child getting ready for school and catching the bus isn't something we would normally celebrate. This is just what we expect. But in order to create a ground where the child feels more seen and acknowledged when not doing anything wrong, we can choose to see and reflect positive steps in the desired direction or any not-negative aspect of that child's getting-ready process as a miracle. The truth is: the child could choose not to budge. How not-great would that be? **So really, in truth, how great is it when things are moving in the right ways?**

IN ORDER TO CREATE A GROUND WHERE THE CHILD FEELS SEEN AND ACKNOWLEDGED WHEN NOT DOING ANYTHING WRONG, WE CAN CHOOSE TO SEE AND REFLECT EVERY POSITIVE OR NOT-NEGATIVE ASPECT OF THAT CHILD'S GETTING-READY PROCESS AS A MIRACLE.

When you consider how *not-great* a morning can become when your child chooses to refuse to get out of bed, shower, get dressed, or eat breakfast, you recognize how *great* every positive step in that regard can be. You can experience real gratitude for even microscopic positive choices.

BREAK IT DOWN AND ADD IT UP

Let's break down the small choices made by the child who gets to school on time. Think in terms of *baby steps,* with each positive choice, movement toward that positive choice, or simple failure to make a negative choice worthy of grateful acknowledgment.

And then, let's add it up: give all the credit and acknowledgement for all these positive choices or absence of negative choices right back to the child.

Another way of describing this process: as a *pixelation* of the everyday realities you experience with your child. Digital images are composed of pixels; imagine that each pixel, when expanded and viewed with an eye to the positive, can be seen as its own small miracle.

BREAK IT DOWN, ADD IT UP: NOAH'S MORNING ROUTINE

To make it to his seat by the first bell, 12-year-old Noah climbs out of his cozy bed by 7:00 AM. Mom has to go into his room three times to get him on his feet, but he gets there. He has to shake off sleep and walk himself to the bathroom to pee. With a few parental prompts, he washes up, combs his hair, and gets dressed in his favorite torn sweats and baggy T-shirt. He wolfs down his breakfast, gathers his homework papers and books and stuffs them into his backpack, says goodbye, puts on his bike helmet, and jumps on his bike and rides to school.

In traditional modes of parenting, we might focus on the difficulty Mom had getting Noah out of bed, his choice of torn sweats, how he wolfed his food down quickly, or the messy way in which he stuffed his things into his backpack. See the problem, talk about the problem, try to solve the problem: that's what most parents instinctively do. The pull to focus on problems is almost gravitational in our world. And sure, Noah could have chosen better in some ways, but let's try focusing, microscopically, on what Noah has done right:

- Getting out of a nice warm bed is challenging for anyone, and the fact that he didn't have to be dragged demonstrates that he has will power and drive, and that he feels considerate toward his mom – he didn't make her come back a fourth time to get him out of bed!

- Washing up suggests that he values cleanliness and good grooming. How *not great* is it when a 12-year-old boy refuses to shower?

- Since Noah's siblings share the bathroom with him, he needed to be cooperative and flexible in his routine when others needed access to that space.

- Picking out his clothes and getting dressed reflects his personal creativity and pride in his appearance. Those holey sweats feel right to him, and he's not so vain that he's concerned about appearance over comfort.

- He got to the breakfast table and ate quickly because he was keeping track of the time, and knew if he went too slowly he would not be able to finish his meal. So he's also being ecologically-minded, not wasteful.

- He remembered all the papers he needed for school and took responsibility for getting them out the door in time. What parent hasn't had to deliver homework or other materials to a kid who forgot to do what Noah did? Not great. So his demonstration of responsibility in remembering those papers is *all kinds of great.* He is being the greatness of thoughtfulness and consideration.

- Being able to safely ride his bike to school means Noah has the awareness and focus needed to follow bike safety protocols. He wears a helmet because he wants to stay safe; he knows his well-being is important to a lot of people.

WHAT IF ... I DON'T HAVE TIME FOR THIS?

This is a common initial reaction to the idea of giving frequent positive recognitions. Consider how much time can be swept into negativity: reactivity, lectures, struggling to gain or maintain control, or feeling anxious, worried or concerned in the heat of the moment or behind the scenes that the train of decent behavior could leave the tracks at any moment. Now, let's add up the actual time you might expect to spend giving these recognitions, with the caveat that there may be a slightly larger time commitment as you get the approach fully launched and convince your child(ren) that things have changed and that energy will no longer be available for negativity. Know that you can't just announce change; you have to create a firsthand experience by consistently *being* the change. Once the approach has deeply settled into your relationship with your child, fewer recognitions will be needed – but you probably won't want to back off once you know how good it feels to relate to your child in this way.

CHAPTER 4

To make miracles from molecules, all that's needed is a firm intention and an open mind and heart. The NHA techniques are designed to give you all you need to share with the child, in the flow of the day, about what you choose to creatively recognize and acknowledge, the beauty you appreciate in this child, and the miracles you see, moment to moment.

Consider This ...

Do you have five minutes a day to shift the trajectory of your child's life and the depth, sweetness and positivity of the relationship you share? Can you imagine giving:

- *Ten recognitions per day taking 30 seconds apiece or less? That's five minutes per day.*

- *Fifteen recognitions per day taking 20 seconds apiece?*

- *Or 20 per day, 15 seconds a piece?*

Also: as you practice and build your skills, you'll get better at "drive-by" recognitions that are short, simple, and profoundly impactful. Howard is fond of saying, "In three minutes a day, you can change your child's life." That's 30 times 10 seconds: 30 quick recognitions of 10 seconds each will have dramatic impact.

This is where we begin to hand out $100 bills for positivity (including the absence of negativity). This is where the child begins to learn that his parents are really connected and present with him when he's just doing his regular life. He no longer has to go to the trouble of conjuring negativity to get engagement; he comes to see that the most important people in his world cherish the thoughtful kindness of his collaborative efforts.

THIS IS WHERE WE BEGIN TO HAND OUT ENERGETIC $100 BILLS FOR POSITIVITY VIA RESPONSE AND RELATIONSHIP, AND WHERE THE CHILD BEGINS TO LEARN THAT HIS PARENTS TRULY SEE AND APPRECIATE HIM WHEN HE'S JUST LIVING HIS REGULAR LIFE.

He doesn't have to bring home awards, trophies or straight As to be seen; neither does he have to break rules and create havoc to be seen.

Noah's parents can choose to direct the talent and artistry required to make a mountain out of a molehill into brilliantly creating miracles from molecules. They convey to Noah that he is profoundly valued. Through this seeing in positivity, they provide ongoing primal nutrition that feeds his soul – and will help him grow in strength and consideration for others.

Challenge

1. Study this photograph. Imagine the scenario. How can not-great inform you about the truth of this moment? In other words, what could be going wrong that isn't?

2. Consider: how not-great would that be; and, therefore, how great is the fact that it isn't happening right now?

3. Feel how this perspective sheds light on the beauty of this child's choices in the moment. Give the child credit for those good choices; remember that most children would certainly get credit for any poor choices!

4. Now, go back to the same photograph. What more is great about this moment? Consider any good choice, movement toward a good choice, neutral choice, or failure to make a bad choice to be fair game.

5. Snap a photo of a few activities or times of day with your child. Later on, sit down with the photo and repeat the exercise above: write out a miracles-from-molecules statement for each photo. Remember to include moments where poor choices are not being made as raw material for greatness recognitions.

ISN'T TOO MUCH PRAISE THE PROBLEM?

During the 2000s, several research studies and books stating that praise has been ruining our kids were published. Throughout that time, those of us aligned with the NHA were unperturbed, because all evidence suggests that the problem is not praise, but the way in which praise is given.

We agree that a certain kind of praise is, at best, unhelpful, and at worst, toxic: generic praise that has no connection to the lived experience of the child being praised. A child who hears "You're awesome!" or "Good job!" or "You're great!" without any context *(How am I awesome? In what way did I do a good job? How do you know I'm great?)* might feel a momentary thrill, but ultimately, such praises don't build inner wealth – especially on a day when the child is feeling the opposite of awesome, good, or great. It's like handing a construction worker a building block made of gelatin: it doesn't support further development.

Those ways of offering praise are well-intended, but they fall flat in terms of convincing a child that he or she is deeply appreciated, valued and meaningful – that he or she is seen on what we would call a "soul level."

The kind of praise we recommend is related directly and specifically to a particular choice the child is making and to the aspects of that child's greatness that are revealed through that choice.

Vague, vacuous praise never quite hits home. It doesn't meet the deep nutritional needs of the heart of the intense child. A surfeit of vague praise is equivalent to too much junk food: it might taste good and satisfy in the moment, but it fails to provide the primal nutrition that builds inner wealth.

Although the average child might feel somewhat seen and acknowledged by non-specific praise, it feels hollow and dishonest to the intense child. That intense child's portfolio is too full of experiences of being seen and connected with most passionately around her wrongdoings. *She needs detailed evidence about her greatness in order to shift the leanings of that portfolio.*

Ever had someone tell you how nice you look on a day when you don't see how it could be possible? We are strongly inclined to dismiss or defend against such praise. Or, have you ever been told that you are being kind when, in your own head, you're replaying moments when you did not see yourself being kind? How authentic do those recognitions feel to you? In most cases, they bounce right off or bring up negative self-talk: "I'm *not* good, I'm *not* attractive or kind." For an intense child, whose "B.S. meter" is naturally stronger because it's based on firsthand experiences of often being in trouble, this impact is magnified.

Think, once more, about how minutely and eloquently we can identify problems, mistakes, and other things we want the child to correct! In making miracles from molecules, we are really only correcting an imbalance – using our skill at talking about what's wrong to talk about what's right.

Intense children have likely received an abundance of attempts to set limits. They have probably often found themselves at the confluence of multiple streams of critical, negative feedback – a great many words that all land the same way: *failure, failure,* and *failure*. No sane, loving person would ever do this to a child on purpose, but it happens inadvertently all the time, especially with intense children by way of normal and traditional approaches to interaction. *Failure* is how children drink in the energy of lectures, reprimands, and normal styles of limit-setting statements like "stop it", "cut it out" and "quit it."

By the time these intense children reach school, they may well have a remarkable accumulation of first-hand experiences that feel like failure. And then, when we go to give these same children a compliment, if all we have at our disposal is "thank you" or good job," it's possible – if not probable – that such a child will dismiss or defend against what we intend. On the inside, they feel a kind of knowing: "That's not true."

A consistent flow of new streams made up of detailed, heartfelt, authentic positive statements, along with a refusal to give any further energy to negativity, is the transformative solution. They may not want to stand at that confluence at first. It may feel strange to them. But as we convert 'thank you' and 'good job' into powerful real-time acknowledgements that open up channels of positivity, the shift will be set in motion.

The NHA techniques give us a format within which to give relationship and energy to a child when the child is *not doing anything wrong,* to take advantage of any those prime moments, and to do it in ways that are highly nutritious and easily 'digestible.'

ACKNOWLEDGEMENTS MUST INCLUDE INFORMATION ABOUT WHY OR HOW THE CHILD IS AWESOME, GREAT, DOING A GOOD JOB, OR COMPELLING YOU TO EXPRESS THE APPRECIATION YOU HAVE FOR THE BEAUTY YOU SEE IN HER…AND, IDEALLY, WILL ALSO INCLUDE SPECIFIC INFORMATION ABOUT WHAT THE GOOD OR GREAT CHOICE SAYS ABOUT THE CHILD MAKING IT.

These recognitions download as true reflections of the child in her greatness. In order for these acknowledgements and reflections to land in a way that boosts inner wealth, they must include information about *why* or *how* the child is being awesome or great, doing a good job, or otherwise compelling you to express your appreciation you have for the beauty you see in her.

Ideally, such praise will also include specific information about what the good or great choice says about the child making it. What qualities of the child's greatness are shining forth as he makes that choice?

TIME IN!

The time-out has become the standard consequence for young children. When bad behavior transpires, parents' general guidelines in popular parenting literature suggest that the child be directed to a special "time-out" spot, where he is expected to spend roughly one minute per year of age. The child is expected to sit quietly, giving both the parent and the child time to calm down; the parent is not supposed to engage the child during that time, unless she leaves the time-out spot. If the child leaves, the parent is supposed to direct the child back to the spot and start the time-out over. If necessary, the parent is supposed to hold the child in the time-out spot so the consequence can be completed. Upon completing the time-out, the parent is instructed to have a brief talk with the child about the transgression, and to remind her that she only has to go to time-out when she breaks a rule.

If you've struggled with time-out along your parenting journey, know that you're not alone! Perhaps the average two-year-old can sit still for two minutes in a time-out. Maybe the average four-year-old can manage four minutes. But when an intense child is in the mix, a successful time-out can feel as elusive as a needle in a haystack. Chances are, along the way, lots of energy and connection will flow to the child for negative choices. Even the prescribed post-time-out "talking to" is perceived by the child as a great dose of you as a result of a poor choice – built-in $100 dollar bills for negativity. Upside-down. It's a setup for a showdown.

Something pivotal is missing: you can't have an effective time-out unless you establish a vital, vibrant time-in – something to miss out on. Getting the energy right-side-up is that pivotal piece to creating a time-in that empowers a time-out that has the impact you have always desired.

You can't create vital and vibrant time-in unless you're already well on your way to demonstrating that you are no longer available through negativity, and that your energies, relationship and connection are now readily available when things are not going wrong. Then, a new form of time-out can work simply and easily.

Traditional time-outs also fail to uphold Stand One. Giving out $100 bills of relationship (energy, emotionally energized connection) in combination with a consequence rewards the child for breaking a rule. Traditional time-outs may be issued reactively and emotionally, with lots of talking about why what happened was wrong or about what should have happened: a handing over of the reward of us in response to a problem. The toys are activated.

In the Nurtured Heart Approach, we utilize a specific kind of time-out called a reset. It resembles the time-out in some very basic ways, but it looks quite different in practice. You learned a bit about the reset in the previous chapter, and much more will be said on that subject in chapters to come. For now, we'll focus on time-in – which, if skillfully and persistently created, will make consequences of any kind less necessary.

Absolutely Yes!
THE SECOND STAND

RELENTLESSLY CREATING AND ENERGIZING POSITIVITY AND SUCCESS - THE NURTURED HEART ENERGIZING TECHNIQUES

CHAPTER OBJECTIVES

- Learn and practice all four NHA energizing techniques: Active Recognition, Experiential Recognition, Proactive Recognition, and Creative Recognition.

- Learn why your house rules should always start with "No."

- Learn to add "qualities of greatness" to your recognitions.

- Begin to see that resistance is not a reason to back down, but to "notch it up."

Now, let's look at the techniques we use in the Nurtured Heart Approach to create a dynamic, exciting and vibrant time-in for your child.

Coupled with an absence of energy to negativity, even the most intense child will come to feel that this time-in is the most interesting, fulfilling place to be.

TECHNIQUE #1: ACTIVE RECOGNITION

To give an Active Recognition, watch the child carefully, and then describe to the child what you see, as though you were describing the scene to a blind person. (Feel free to include the other senses in your descriptions, too!) Do this only when the child is not breaking any rules. Use your "Miracles from Molecules" skills to notice and acknowledge the child in moments when all is well.

Active Recognitions begin with lead-ins like "I see…" "I hear…" "I notice…" "Here's what I'm sensing…" or even "Sounds like…" or "Seems to me like…" Be creative; use any lead-in that opens up the flow of profound noticing. Examples:

"Sarah, I notice you are sitting quietly in the back seat with your brother and it seems like you're looking out the window at the scenery."

"Kevin, I hear you making all kinds of truck sounds while you play trucks with your friend. It's almost like music and they are coming to life through you."

Also use Active Recognitions to capture the child in a moment where he is feeling strong emotions, but is not acting out or harming others:

"Will, I notice you're getting frustrated with your homework assignment…and you're still in your chair, doing your best to figure it out. Frustration can be overwhelming and I see you handling your strong feelings well."

"Jose, I hear you talking to your friend in a voice that seems angry, and I see in your body that you're wanting to grab that toy back from her. I can tell you're feeling some powerful feelings. You're still just using your words, though. It's inspiring to see you managing your big emotions!"

This technique is simple, but profound in its impact. Just seeing and capturing a child in moments where nothing is going wrong provides that child with powerful, in-the-moment evidence that they matter to the adults around them more when they are not breaking rules – especially when these recognitions are coupled with a strong commitment to Stand One.

Challenge

1. For each of the photos above, write a few Active Recognitions.

2. Commit to giving your child/ren at least ten Active Recognitions a day for at least the next two days before moving on to learning and practicing the next technique.

To the child, simply being noticed and acknowledged feels like thirst-quenching recognition. Active Recognitions are especially digestible for teens, who may resist more detailed acknowledgements; or for any child for whom more frankly positive comments may bring up doubt and pushback in the beginning.

WHAT IF...MY CHILD DOES NOT RESPOND WELL TO THESE RECOGNITIONS?

This is a common concern for parents just starting out with the NHA. Parents worry that their children might construe the recognitions as weird or overbearing. For intense, challenging children who are used to being scolded and lectured for misdeeds and largely unacknowledged when doing nothing wrong, this new dynamic can feel disorienting and foreign.

Some children have experienced comments that resonate as sabotaging, hurtful, or sarcastic at some level in moments where they are successful: "So you finally put away your laundry. I'd better buy a lottery ticket, because this must be my lucky day!" Kids used to this or other kinds of unaligned or off-kilter feedback might rail against a sudden hail of positive recognitions that are energetically congruent, especially when heir dance around energy for negativity is no longer working (which it isn't, if the parent skillfully enacts the First Stand).

If the child confronts your use of positive comments in any way, address it without energizing negativity: "You know, I just realized that I spend a lot more energy noticing and talking about what's wrong and your bad choices. So I made a commitment to myself to talk only about what you do right. I know it must feel weird right now. It's a little weird for me too! But I trust we'll both get used to it. That's just how it's going to be from now on, unless I slip up – and if I do, I'm going to reset and remind myself of my commitment as quick as I can and get back to noticing what is going well."

Most children, particularly intense children, push back in some way when these techniques are introduced. This is not a bad turn of events; *when you put a new roof on your house, you want it to rain.* As the child resists and probes for the old dynamic and the parent doesn't relent, the real shift starts. The more a child pushes back or resists positive acknowledgements and withdrawal of energy for negativity, the more acutely the child is likely to need even higher levels of nourishing recognition.

THE MORE A CHILD PUSHES BACK OR RESISTS POSITIVE ACKNOWLEDGEMENTS AND WITHDRAWAL OF ENERGY FOR NEGATIVITY, THE MORE ACUTELY THE CHILD IS LIKELY TO NEED EVEN HIGHER LEVELS OF NOURISHING RECOGNITION.

Resistance is strong evidence that what you are doing is working. It's hitting home. The child who tests to see if it's a fluke wants to know whether you will stand your ground and keep up this new way of noticing and nourishing...or wilt and lose your footing when tested. Hold on to your Stands like you would cling to a life raft in a stormy sea. Rather than letting them go when you encounter resistance, *notch them up* – give them more energy and more commitment. Match the child's intensity. Remember that you can always revert to Active Recognitions, as these simple, incontrovertibly true observations bring up less resistance than the other techniques described in this chapter.

Noticing and giving words to what comes up that doesn't cross the line of a rule being broken will register, for the child, as a further sense of being seen and heard – and can actually land as a successful experience. For example:

"Josh, I hear that you think my comments are weird, and I appreciate that you are letting me know that without yelling or fussing."

"Kay, I notice you look very annoyed by my compliments. I am really appreciating that you able to convey that without words or actions that would make things worse."

"Veronica, I sense that you want me to go away and leave you alone... and yet, as mad as you are because of my compliments, you are allowing the space for me to express myself."

Eventually, the child will recognize that you won't do the old energy-for-negativity dance with him anymore. He'll see that pushing back doesn't get him the fireworks he wants; that he now gets those fireworks for doing well; and that when he breaks rules, all he gets is a short, un-energized reset (more on this in Chapter Six). Eventually, he'll see that the least boring (and, eventually, increasingly exciting) alternative is to learn the new dance.

TECHNIQUE #2: EXPERIENTIAL RECOGNITION

With this technique, we add to Active Recognitions an additional comment about what the child's behavior reveals about her character. In the Nurtured Heart Approach, we refer to desired character qualities as *qualities of greatness*. Actions that reflect, express, or otherwise convey those qualities are recognized not as fleeting or extrinsic, but as absolutely integral and intrinsic to the child's being. "I see/hear/notice you [action/emotion] and here is how that shows me your [quality of greatness]…" Through this practice of greatness recognition, we get to express the qualities of character we are admiring, *right now*. The adult gets to convey this recognition back to the child in a way that expresses the adult's appreciation and credits the child's most basic nature for the greatness that's occurring. The adult is conveying to the child a firsthand experience of *being* those qualities and that aspect of their greatness.

What do you see and hear the child doing – again, when nothing is going wrong? What does this say about who the child is?

Particularly for intense and difficult children, we usually attempt to teach life skills or values in the midst of issues and problems. The child makes a mistake and adults launch into a lecture, reprimand, consequence or pep talk designed to teach the child about the value in question.

Values like honesty, integrity, respect, responsibility, adaptability, balance, candor, individuality, thriftiness, or generosity are great guides toward happy lives and healthy relationships. But the moment where a child is captured in the midst of failing to express those values *is not* the best teaching moment! It is likely to deepen their existing energetic impression that they get more juicy relationship when things are going wrong. They are more likely to defend reactively in the midst of our reactivity or attempts to deliver yet another world-class lecture; they are less likely to hear what we most want to convey in those heated moments. The child is not likely to thank you for your soliloquy, no matter how stunning and inspiring it might be.

In contrast, the most effective way to teach values is *in the moments where they are being expressed*. That is where the child's openness lies.

Here are examples of Experiential Recognitions, built from the Active Recognitions in the first section:

"Sarah, I notice you are sitting quietly in the backseat with your brother. You're looking out the window at the scenery. You are being so calm, kind and thoughtful right now."

"Kevin, I hear you making truck sounds while you play trucks with your friend. You are being imaginative."

"Will, I notice you're getting frustrated with your homework assignment…and you're still in your chair, doing your best to figure it out. You're showing a lot of self-control and discipline."

"Jose, I hear you talking to your friend in a voice that seems angry, and I see in your body that you're wanting to grab that toy back from her. Great job managing your big emotions! You're feeling them all the way and you are showing the respect and skillfulness to put the energy of those feelings toward using your words. I appreciate these great choices."

While Active Recognitions capture the child in moments of success, Experiential Recognitions teach values and good choices through the experience of being applauded for making them. They insert the child into a first-hand experience of being and living that quality.

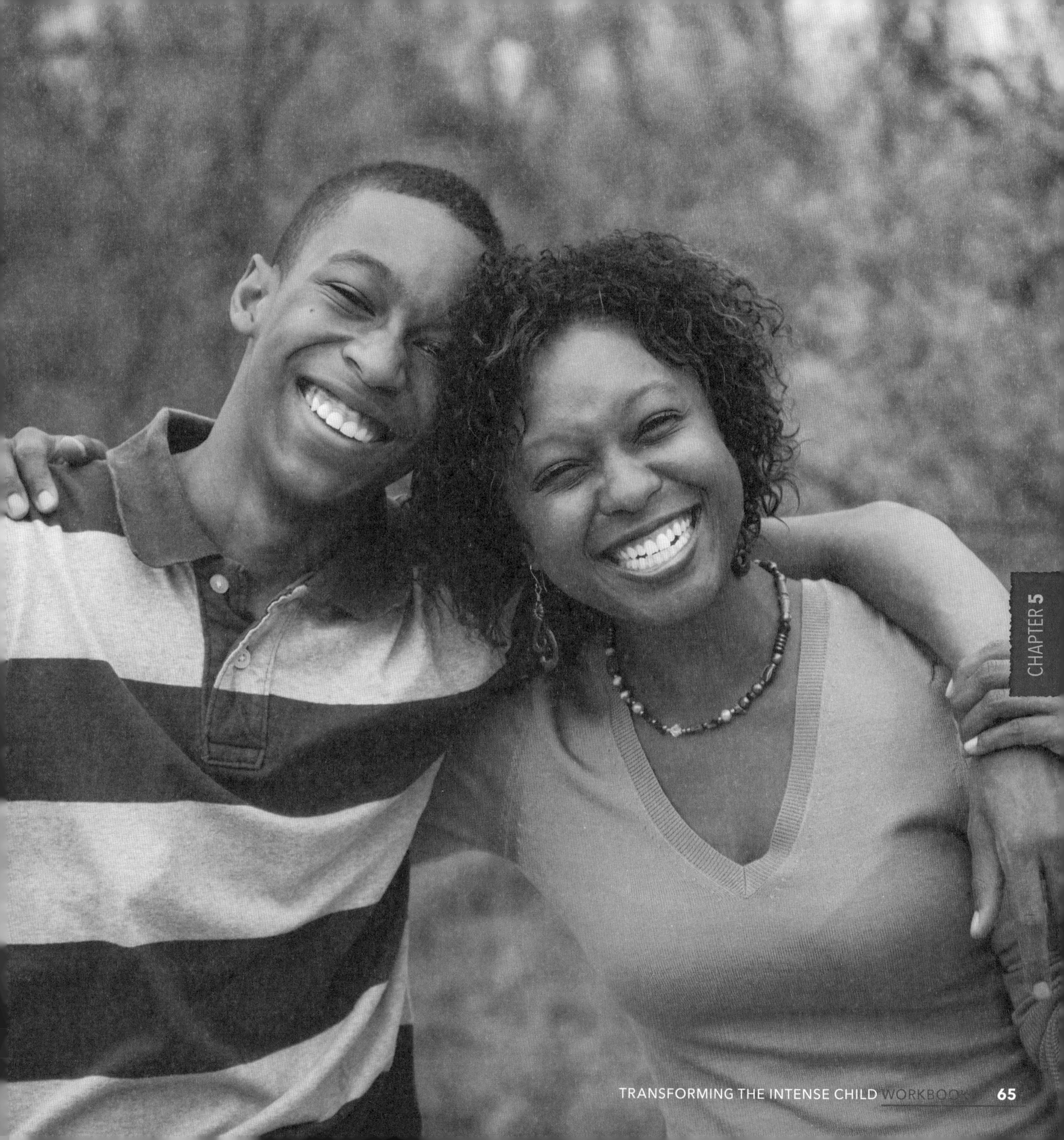

CHAPTER 5

QUALITIES OF GREATNESS: A NON-COMPREHENSIVE LIST*

Use this list as a starting point for Experiential Recognitions. No such list could capture every expression possible through the heart, so allow your own versions to freely flow. Compliments of this nature will flow with authenticity when you let your heart have a voice.

You might post this list in a prominent place to aid your natural adeptness in deriving experiential recognitions. Every time you pass by it, you might choose a quality to energize the next time you and your child are together. Consult it when you aren't sure what word to use to reflect your child's greatness in the moment.

Most of all: consult your heart. You'll be amazed at how you can almost always find a way to see most any one of these qualities being expressed by your child.

Acceptance	Calmness	Contentment	Diversity	Family
Abundance	Candor	Continuity	Dominance	Fascination
Accomplishment	Capability	Contribution	Drive	Fearlessness
Accountability	Care	Control	Duty	Ferocity
Accuracy	Celebrity	Conviction	Dynamism	Fidelity
Achievement	Certainty	Cooperation	Eagerness	Independence
Adaptability	Charity	Courage	Ease	Flexibility
Adoration	Charm	Courtesy	Ecological	Flow
Adventure	Cheerfulness	Craftiness	Economy	Focus
Affection	Clarity	Creativity	Efficiency	Frankness
Agility	Cleanliness	Credibility	Elegance	Freedom
Alertness	Cleverness	Cunning	Eloquence	Friendliness
Altruism	Closeness	Curiosity	Empathy	Friendship
Appreciation	Comfort	Daring	Encouragement	Frugality
Approachability	Commitment	Decisiveness	Endurance	Fun
Artistry	Community	Delight	Energy	Generosity
Assertiveness	Compassion	Dependability	Enjoyment	Giving
Attentiveness	Competence	Depth	Entertainment	Grace
Attractiveness	Completion	Determination	Enthusiasm	Gratitude
Audacity	Composure	Devotion	Excellence	Growth
Availability	Concentration	Dexterity	Excitement	Guidance
Awareness	Confidence	Dignity	Exhilaration	Happiness
Balance	Conformity	Diligence	Expertise	Harmony
Beauty	Congruency	Direction	Exploration	Health
Bliss	Connection	Directness	Expressiveness	Heart
Boldness	Consciousness	Discipline	Exuberance	Helpfulness
Bravery	Conservation	Discovery	Fairness	Heroism
Buoyancy	Consistency	Discretion	Faith	Honesty

Honor
Hopefulness
Hospitality
Humility
Humor
Imagination
Impact
Individuality
Ingenuity
Inquisitiveness
Insightfulness
Inspiration
Integrity
Intelligence
Intensity
Intimacy
Introspection
Intuition
Intuitiveness
Inventiveness
Joy
Judiciousness
Justice
Keenness
Kindness
Knowledge
Leadership
Learning
Lightness
Liveliness
Logic
Longevity
Love
Loyalty
Mastery
Maturity
Meaning
Mellowness
Meticulousness
Mindfulness
Modesty

Motivation
Neatness
Noncomformity
Obedience
Open-mindedness
Optimism
Order
Organization
Originality
Outrageousness
Patience
Passion
Peace
Perceptiveness
Perfection
Perseverance
Persistence
Persuasiveness
Playfulness
Pleasantness
Potency
Power
Practicality
Pragmatism
Precision
Preparedness
Presence
Pride
Privacy
Proactivity
Punctuality
Rationality
Realism
Reason
Reasonableness
Recognition
Recreation
Refinement
Reflection
Relaxation
Reliability

Relief
Resilience
Resolution
Resolve
Resourcefulness
Respect
Responsibility
Restraint
Reverence
Richness
Rigor
Satisfaction
Security
Self-care
Self-control
Selflessness
Self-reliance
Self-respect
Sensitivity
Serenity
Service
Sharing
Shrewdness
Silliness
Simplicity
Sincerity
Skillfulness
Solidarity
Solitude
Speed
Spirituality
Spontaneity
Spunk
Stability
Status
Stealth
Stillness
Strength
Structure
Success
Support

Surprise
Sympathy
Teamwork
Thankfulness
Thoroughness
Thoughtfulness
Thrift
Tranquility
Transcendence
Trust
Trustworthiness
Understanding
Unflappability
Uniqueness
Unity
Valor
Vigor
Vision
Vitality
Vivacity
Warmth
Watchfulness
Wisdom
Wittiness
Wonder
Zeal

Challenge

Write or speak three Experiential Recognitions for each of these images. Use the list of qualities of greatness as needed.

Catching children being congruent, intrepid, or intuitive is a wonderful opportunity to teach them new words in a way that they feel in their bones. If I'm engaged in a project and I'm told that I am being meticulous, diligent, resourceful, or wise in my attention to detail, I will integrate that word into my experience of myself and I'll likely never forget it... especially if I am given a clear context and incontrovertible evidence.

Our Best Advice/Words of Encouragement...

With Experiential Recognitions:

1. *Make it your mission to see the beauty of your child's choices during times when problems are not happening. Let your heart guide you in giving expression to the attributes that contribute to those choices: wisdom, compassion, thoughtfulness, kindness. Inhabit the words. Your compliments are more than words; they are a full expression of YOU!*

2. *Choose to give lectures about how respect is happening in the moments when your child is getting along and being respectful and being responsible. Let her know how much you appreciate those choices.*

3. *Make it your mission to give abundant detailed evidence in support of your apppreciative comments. The detail and sincerity of your recognition creates a first-hand experience of the empowerment of "time-in."*

GREATNESS RECOGNITIONS

The test of leadership is not to put greatness into humanity, but to elicit it, for the greatness is already there. – James Buchanan

In our book *Igniting Greatness,* we say that greatness is "in our birthright and in our hardware." A seed becomes a plant; an acorn becomes a tree; a flower becomes a fruit. Within those beginnings lies all the greatness of the thing that grows from it. So it is with us: each human being is endowed with greatness. Nurtured Heart appreciations are designed to awaken a sense of one's own intrinsic greatness – not as something that comes about through hard work only or pure luck of the draw, but as something we all possess.

The passage in *Igniting Greatness* continues: "The challenges we *think* we face are *self-improvement, boosting self-esteem,* maybe being a higher achiever, competing better in the rat race of life, improving relationships with specific people in our lives, or finding the relationship, livelihood or self-definition that might make us feel just *okay* about who we are. The true challenge we came to meet was that of simply remembering the greatness we brought with us into this world."

What if we began to see our primary task as parents, educators and caregivers as inspiring our children to remember this greatness? We would light up the runway for them as they activated, owned and explored this greatness for themselves.

WHAT IF WE SAW OUR PRIMARY TASK AS INSPIRING OUR CHILDREN TO REMEMBER THEIR GREATNESS?

What if we had faith that an active focus on awakening greatness was really the key thing children needed from us to thrive and blossom? If we believed that this ground of greatness would provide the child with every resource necessary – including the inner wealth and the social-emotional intelligence required for a happy and productive life? Wouldn't parenting and teaching get a lot simpler?

We believe, with all our hearts, that this is a truth about parenting and teaching. The simple recognitions you've learned thus far will get you started; now, let's look at how you can tailor these recognitions to help the child see his positive and neutral choices as expressions of his greatness.

"Sarah, I notice you are sitting quietly in the backseat with your brother. You're looking out the window at the scenery. You have the greatness of calm and inner reflection."

See the nuance? We're identifying these qualities of calm and inner reflection as immovable aspects of who Sarah is.

"Kevin, I hear you making truck sounds while you play trucks with your friend. You have the greatness of imagination and creativity!"

"Will, I notice you're getting frustrated with your homework assignment…and you're still in your chair, doing your best to figure it out. Your greatness of self-control and discipline are really shining through right now."

"Jose, I hear you talking to your friend in a voice that seems angry, and I see in your body that you might want to grab that toy back from her…You haven't done that. You haven't screamed, yelled, or used bad words. You have the greatness of steadiness, clear communication and intention to be a wonderful friend."

The linguistic constructions required to verbally call out greatness might not jive too well with the *Chicago Manual of Style*. Some adults feel resistant to using the same word (greatness) over and over again. For those willing to move past such resistance or grammatical perfectionism, there is the reward of almost magical impact.

One night, coauthor Melissa waited in the wings of a small performance venue to perform an original piece of solo choreography. Her heart pounded and her stomach churned with the worst stage fright she'd ever experienced. Desperate for relief, she began to jump up and down in place and say to herself, over and over: "Greatness. Greatness. Greatness. Greatness..." This calmed her and helped her to recognize that her entire reason for being there, that night, was to share greatness and to inspire others to feel this in themselves.

The word can become an incantation that eventually stands on its own: a reminder to remember who we really are; that we are, at our ground, created in greatness. We are safe in that truth. We might stray into negativity or problem orientation, but a growing GPS of greatness can always lead us back to a better place. What a gift to give to a child – especially the child who has faced challenges.

Challenge

1. Observe your child carefully to inspire Experiential Recognitions of your own. Write them out, and then modify them to create greatness recognitions. Practice saying them out loud with your co-parent, colleague or friends. The more you practice, the more easily these recognitions will come.

2. Set a goal to give your child 10 Experiential Recognitions a day for two days before moving on to the next technique.

TECHNIQUE #3: PROACTIVE RECOGNITION

In traditional modes of parenting, we tend to talk with energy about the rules only when they're broken or about to be broken. In the Nurtured Heart Approach, rules provide vast potential for positive recognitions – because any rule not being broken is a great opportunity for Inner Wealth-building acknowledgement and celebration of the greatness that choice represents.

---

*ANY RULE **NOT** BEING BROKEN IS A GREAT OPPORTUNITY FOR INNER WEALTH-BUILDING ACKNOWLEDGEMENT AND CELEBRATION OF THE GREATNESS THAT CHOICE REPRESENTS.*

While any moment where a child is not doing anything wrong is fair game for Proactive Recognition, these recognitions are especially potent when given to a child who may be moving toward breaking a rule, but hasn't yet crossed the line.

In simplest terms, the formula for Proactive Recognition is:

APPRECIATION OF RULE NOT BROKEN

+

EXPERIENTIAL RECOGNITION

(with greatness recognitions where they feel right)

For a toddler: "Timothy, I see the great choice you are making. You're not pouring your cup of milk on the floor! You're being helpful, following our rule about not making a big mess on purpose while we eat our snack!"

For a preschooler: "SiJie, thanks so much for not grabbing that toy out of Celeste's hands. I can see how much you want it back, and you're doing a great job of following our no-grabbing rule – that is such good self-control."

For an elementary-aged child and older: "John, you didn't break the no-interrupting rule with the grown-ups when they were talking. You waited until we were done. That shows me you have the greatness of patience and respect."

For a high schooler: "Kimberly, thank you for coming home sober. I sense that some of your friends were probably drinking, and they might have pressured you to join them. You kept your promise to me about not drinking, and that shows me your honesty, integrity, and willpower. Those are great qualities I see in you. And you look like you still had fun, which makes me respect you for knowing how to have a good time without drinking."

The reality is that a child can choose to break a rule at any time. If you've been dealing with a difficult child, you know this all too well, as do they, and perhaps you've gone through many emotional ups and downs around not having more control in this realm. The flip side of this is that *every time a child does not break a rule that, too, is a choice.* It is a choice for which the child can be given credit. It is a choice that can be used to further illuminate the child's greatness. *And the reality is that most of the time, even the most challenging child isn't breaking any rules.*

EVERY TIME A CHILD DOES NOT BREAK A RULE, THIS IS A CHOICE - A CHOICE FOR WHICH THE CHILD CAN BE GIVEN CREDIT.

Notice that the rules acknowledged in these examples are generally stated in the negative: No making a mess; no grabbing things out of other people's hands; no interrupting adults when they are talking. This may go against your conception of the best way to give rules. Most "positive parenting" approaches state that rules should be stated in positive language: *Keep your space neat. Keep your hands to yourself.* Most parents and teachers will state rules in this way; it's become the cultural norm.

The problem with positive rules is that they're unclear and imprecise. The lines are fuzzy. If the lines around a sports field were staggered or zigzagged, the referee's ability to be precise, both when rules are broken and in seeing the beauty of rules not broken, would be undermined.

A positive rule like "be kind" or "be respectful" makes it that much harder to discern when the child has crossed the threshold into being unkind or disrespectful. It's that much harder to tell when the foot is on the line. If a child appeared to be ready to call a classmate names, and *almost* did it, but at the last minute restrained herself...isn't that a victory? How not-great would it be if that child did name-call, or worse – so then how great is it that they exercised restraint?

Clear rules allow for much more opportunity to see the beauty of positive choices to follow the rules.

Consider This ...

Consider the rule "be respectful." Have you ever had a child roll his eyes or say something questionable that gave you pause to wonder: was the rule broken or was it not broken? Meanwhile, the child drinks in your confusion, riveted to it as though it were a neon sign, waiting for you to crack; and the really intense child, seeing that you don't know how to respond, is more likely than not to take it up a notch.

This is not a child out to ruin your life. This is a child brilliantly fishing for two things: 1. connection, and 2. clarity. What he is really hoping is that the rule will materialize in a way that finally makes sense. What he most wants is to know where exactly the line is between rule followed and rule broken. That is why we strongly recommend your rules start with "no." Either the foot is on the line or over the line (rule broken) or behind it, maybe even close but yet not touching it (rule followed!). With that clarity, you have much greater exactitude in knowing whether a violation has occurred.

As long as the rule has not been broken, keep cheering. If the child reels himself in and doesn't break the rule, give him credit! Consider how willing most adults are to give children heaps of acknowledgement when lines are crossed and rules are broken. Give equally great detailed recognition for restraint when lines are not crossed.

As soon as the rule is broken, there is no need for anything other than a reset - no lecture, no meltdown, and no inadvertent $100 bills of reactivity or relationship.

Normal attempts to enforce rules so often backfire because this currency of connection is usually given in the midst of limit-setting. Clear rules set the stage to have great impact in this pivotal realm, especially when this clarity leads us to express appreciation of rules that could have been broken, but weren't. Now the current is flowing in the great direction of inner wealth.

Parenting experts stated in recent years that parents should say "no" as seldom as possible. The Nurtured Heart Approach says "no" to that! When appropriately used to draw clear boundaries, the word "no" is enormously valuable and empowering, especially for children who are addicted to pushing limits. Without a calm, grounded "no," there can be no real "yes." Hopefully, you've already experienced the power of no through the First Stand. Here, it supports you in compassionately, clearly energizing a child for not breaking rules, and will support you when it comes time for you to master the reset used every time a rule is broken.

With the average kid, who won't as strongly seek energy for negativity, positive rules might work, as such children have an innate desire to stay on the side of the line where they aren't in trouble. They'll tend to interpret positive rules in the way adults intend. An intense kid will play near, on, and just to the far side of that line – *especially* if he intuits that his parents are strongly emotionally invested in him *not* breaking the rules. For these children, positive rules are a gilded invitation to thrash all over the line to see what gets the energetic $100 bills flowing.

FOR THE INTENSE CHILD, POSITIVE RULES ARE A GILDED INVITATION TO THRASH ALL OVER THE LINE TO SEE WHAT GETS THE ENERGETIC $100 BILLS FLOWING.

This is not to say that non-intense children won't benefit from negative rules. The gift, for those children, is the vast increase in potential for acknowledgements. Do you think that "good" children get tired of feeling unseen for following the rules? Have you noticed how such children can feel cheated when the challenging kids get so much more relational bandwidth from adults? Giving Proactive Recognitions across the board, to all kids, helps level that playing field, because all children can be recognized with equal verve and appreciation for the rules they are not breaking.

Our Best Advice/Words of Encouragement...

Never give Nurtured Heart recognitions to a child who is breaking a rule!
As you develop your skills in resetting your child/ren according to Stand Three, these techniques will equip you to jump on the first opportunities to bring the child back to time-in. You can do this at the instant the broken rule is no longer being violated.

Until then, simply withhold your energy in the midst of rule-breaking, and look for the first opportunity to give it again in response to something positive. In this way you will be moving strongly in the new direction of great positive impact.

The goals:

- To build within the child a progressing sense of successfulness, and to demonstrate to the child that you see her ongoing choices to not break rules as expressions of her greatness.

- To be truly proactive. Why wait until a rule is broken to take on the role of teaching it? Insert the intended lesson proactively during the time of the child's greatest receptivity: when the rule is being followed. For example, let the child who is quite capable of arguing – but who is not currently arguing – know you appreciate her using her power and wisdom to make her current choice.

Challenge

The first step for creating solid Proactive Recognitions is to list the rules you expect children to follow. If you have been stating your rules in the positive, re-word them so that they all begin with "No..." You may find that you have many more rules when you re-write them in this way than you did when stating rules more positively. This makes sense, because those old positive rules covered a lot more ground – and they lacked the specificity required to make effective limit setting work.

A few examples to get you going:

INSTEAD OF:	*TRY:*
Be respectful.	No interrupting others. No rude gestures. No insulting others. No smartphone use while others are in the room.
Keep your hands to yourself.	No hurting others' bodies with your body. No hitting. No kicking. No pushing.
Be honest.	No lying. No cheating. No stealing.
Keep our home neat and tidy.	No leaving clothing on the floor. No leaving dirty dishes in your room. No leaving trash where it doesn't belong.

Create your own list, either with old and new versions of rules or with a fresh-start new-list version.

As you craft your rules, keep in mind that the point (for now) is to create as much inspiration for Proactive Recognitions as possible.

You can always add more rules on the fly; for now, make your list as comprehensive as you can. The more rules, the better. Through these recognitions, rules become gifts. They propel you to see and appreciate the truth of the child not breaking the rules. As the child finds herself recognized for *not* fussing, *not* arguing, and *not* defying, she comes to see rules as friends, not enemies.

SHOULD YOU POST YOUR NEW LIST OF RULES?

You can, but you don't need to. Lists on the wall are only that until they come alive through your reflections of your appreciation and gratitude for when they are not being broken. As long as *you* are crystal-clear on the rules, your commitment to:

1. not energizing them when they are broken,

2. acknowledging the child often for not breaking rules, and

3. resetting the child every time a rule is broken (more on that in Chapter Six)
   …is what matters most in terms of making this approach work its magic.

Challenge

1. Write or speak two Proactive Recognitions for each photo.

2. Give at least 10 Proactive Recognitions to your children in the next two days.

CREATIVE RECOGNITION

What parent hasn't seen a request turn into a knock-down, drag-out war with an oppositional child? Not a fun situation. By now, you understand why a child will refuse even the simplest request ("Would you finish your homework, please?" "Can you go brush your teeth?" "Please pick up your room"), even if the adult is requesting that he do something he really doesn't mind doing. Fewer things get the fireworks and intense connection going faster than a refusal to comply with an adult's request. In this final of the four NHA techniques, we use clear requests to create inroads to powerful recognitions of greatness and new patterns of cooperation and collaboration.

Our favorite story regarding this technique came from an exhausted father of a highly oppositional child who, initially, couldn't imagine catching his challenging son in a moment of success. He came back to Howard glowing, as though he'd just won a bet.

*"We were getting in the car to go somewhere," he said, "and my son was closing the car door after climbing in. 'I need you to close the door,' I said, and when it closed, I turned around and said, 'Thanks for closing the door. I really appreciate that you followed my directions and did what I asked you to do.'" The child would have had to aggressively reverse the action in order to **not** comply.*

"That's a home run," Howard told the father, seeing how he'd set the stage for success to occur and highlighted it with appreciation as it unfolded.

"And then," the father said, "when I heard him pulling his seatbelt on and it was about to click, I asked him to put his seatbelt on...and when it clicked, I thanked him in a very detailed way for following directions and for making a great choice to be cooperative."

"That was a grand slam home run," Howard told him.

By way of this father's creativity in making clear, utterly doable requests, and by combining those requests with explicit appreciations for movement in the new direction of collaboration and cooperation, just two weeks later this previously highly defiant, uncooperative child could be told, "I need you to start your homework," or "I need you to get ready for bed," and the child would change gears immediately and do what was asked - even if those requests came in the middle of a fun activity like watching TV or playing a video game.

Andrew Lever / Shutterstock.com

With Creative Recognition, the adult creatively makes cooperation and collaboration a reality by 'hijacking' a child into a ready-made opportunity for success. They make a clear request to the child to perform a task that he or she is about to perform, or is in the process of performing, or makes a request in some way that is impossible for the child to resist. The child is then recognized for all the greatness expressed in making that choice. We give the child all the credit; more specifically, we give all the credit to the child's greatness.

Notice how this father made his request: "I need you to…" Avoid giving the child any sense of having an option to *not* comply: "Would you?..." "Could you please?..." "Can you?..." "Will you?..." Instead, go with a statement of your need for the child to do something. Soft starts may seem more polite, and we may want to model politeness for our children; but making requests this way implies an option and will tempt challenging children to veer into non-compliance in hopes of gaining juicier connectivity. A request like this won't end in a question mark, but with a period:

I need you to let the dog out.

I want you to empty the dishwasher.

Go ahead and put the chalk in the drawer.

Creative Recognitions shift the old dynamic of "a request followed + refusal to comply = super juicy connection and lots of interesting reactivity from my favorite toy" to "my cooperation and compliance get me all the connection I need."

Challenge

1. Think through the course of your day with your child. Identify and list four points in the day where you could give Creative Recognition around something the child normally does.

2. Write down the situation and the recognition you plan to give. If you have more than one child, do this exercise for each child. Be as creative as necessary in making these a reality. You are literally stealing opportunities to create these successes as you make headway and change the energy of stuck relationship.

3. Over the course of the next two days, give these Creative Recognitions (along with continued Active, Experiential and Proactive Recognitions).

RECOGNITIONS FROM THE HEART

These four techniques for upholding Stand Two are about pointing out to the child:

- Here is what IS HAPPENING that can be applauded.

- Here is what is NOT HAPPENING that can be applauded.

- Here is what these things reveal to me about your greatness.

Once you have all the techniques up and running, begin to use them in combination. As you allow yourself to experiment and play, know that in the first few weeks of working with this, you may feel awkward.

These appreciations may bring up issues within you, especially if you've never been appreciated in these ways. To those coming from a lineage where positive connection has been rare, the NHA techniques may feel strange, scary, unfounded, or exhilarating. As you reset, remind yourself that what you are really doing here is fighting for your child's life. These techniques will make all the difference in the world in creating the relationship with your child that you always wanted and sensed was possible. Reset as often as needed to stay the course.

The techniques may, at first, feel mechanical or stilted. When you have this sense, see if you can reset yourself to a sense of your positive statements coming straight from your heart.

Whenever you reset yourself or need a moment to come up with recognition, breathe right into the center of your chest and bring yourself into a place of complete presence with the child. Remember your ultimate intention: to be connected in a positive way with this young person and to help her see and live from her own greatness.

Remember the Baby Steps intention: recognize the miraculous in the everyday. Remember how *not-great* it is when the child breaks rules. Let that remembering foster deep gratitude for the absence of rule-breaking and for whatever successes or movement toward success you see in this moment. Know that on the other side of the awkwardness lies the relationship you truly want to have with your child.

Consider This ...

Emotional management, growth and responsibility are tough, even for most adults - let alone children who are just coming into their own in terms of grappling with powerful feelings and developing the wisdom and inner strength required to handle strong internal pushes and pulls.

Challenging feelings like anger, fear, remorse or anxiety can be especially difficult for an intense child to manage, and can lead to the child acting out or being self-destructive. The NHA techniques offer a simple, potent modality for improving emotional management by recognizing a child for all the incremental movements she makes toward managing emotions well; for stopping herself in the midst of a tailspin; and for expressing emotions in healthy ways.

Let's say your child is stressed almost to the breaking point while studying for an exam. The child is clearly headed for a meltdown. You could try giving a pep talk ("You can do this! I believe in you!"), an attempt to rescue ("Maybe we can put off the test, or I can help you study"), or warn the child not to let her emotions get the best of her ("You know you always do this, and you know it's not helpful, so knock it off"). All these engage relationship with negativity and imply, to varying degrees, that the child is not successful in this moment. Even the most well-intended pep talk carries the energetic implication that, apparently, the child is not handling this well.

CHAPTER 5

*Instead, use NHA recognitions to capture her in moments where she is stressed, frustrated or upset, but managing it or pulling herself out of it to varying degrees. The task is in creatively finding moments of success - even those that, at first, seem random - and pointing to these pivotally as Horse Whisperer moments: "**Here you are, doing** it." This is you handling your strong feelings well and you are appreciated for your efforts. These incremental successes plant the seeds that grow into skillfulness, emotional confidence, and competence.*

"I can see you're really anxious about this test, and you're staying put in your seat and continuing to study! That shows me how focused and disciplined you are. Anxiety is a hard emotion to feel and you're managing it really well."

USE NHA RECOGNITIONS TO CAPTURE YOUR CHILD IN MOMENTS WHERE SHE IS STRESSED, FRUSTRATED OR UPSET, BUT MANAGING OR EVEN PULLING HERSELF OUT OF IT.

"Just then I saw you were about to give up, and you didn't! I think I saw you take a couple of deep breaths and close your eyes to give yourself a moment to reset and re-focus. That's wonderful self-care...I'm seeing you beautifully rally your inner strength, Jessica."

"Josh, I saw you being picked on by those other kids and telling them to leave you alone. Then I saw you walk away, and it looked like you were frustrated, maybe a little angry and sad. First of all, I love that you tried using your words; and then, when they didn't listen, I love that you used your wisdom and power to walk away. You didn't break rules or lash out or cause more problems. Instead, you chose to handle your strong feelings beautifully. I love the maturity you are showing in handling challenging situations."

A child spoken to in this way about tough emotional states is having a direct experience of all emotions being acceptable; of parents or teachers who don't fear strong emotion or its expression; and of adults who value them for living their strengths.

A Creative Recognition can even help a child try something new to express or deal with a tough emotion. Let's say the child is welling up with tears and starting to get up to walk away from the study station. "It looks like you're sensing that your anxiety is too big right now for you to stay put and keep studying. I'm gathering that you're on your way to take care of yourself. Great work being discerning and choosing how to manage your stress."

Our Best Advice/Words of Encouragement...

In those moments where you are energizing the child for handling tough emotions, it isn't about the test or the grade. It's about the child being able to sit with discomfort and not act out.

You are showing your child who she really is as someone who has this capacity. It's not a question of whether she can or can't – she *is* choosing to handle her stress constructively.

For every incident where the child *does* act out because of emotional discomfort, there is usually a buildup. If you can watch for that buildup and capture the child in moments of feeling deeply but not acting out, you can quickly give that child an honest impression that she is good at emotional management and can handle more adversity than she ever believed she could. You can provide this proof for him that it's not a question of whether he can or can't; he *is* handling it well, right now.

THE MORE INTENSE THE CHILD, THE MORE INTENSE THE NHA APPLICATION

Over the years, many parents have reached out to Howard to ask for consultations or coaching directly from the NHA's founder. They've tried their best on their own, they say, and it's just not working – the child is either unchanged or escalating. Howard's usual initial response: "Sure, I'll consult with you, but first I need you to apply the approach *as though your life depended on it* for the next month. Also, put all other approaches aside during this period of time. Use this one only, so we can dial it in its purest form and I can truly see where I can best be of service. Then, if it still isn't working, I'll step in."

In every case, the parents find they don't require direct help. They just needed an extra push to help their application of the approach match the intensity of their child.

Always keep this in mind as you work with the approach: the more intense the child, the more intense the application of the approach required. Hold tight to your Stands and notch it up until the desired impact is seen. Refuse more staunchly to energize negativity; amp up the positives; get clearer about the rules - a process we call "notching it up" that we will address in more detail later in this workbook.

For now, be watchful of what levels of appreciation are most impactful.

Reach as deeply as needed into your purpose and your intention. Let the form of these Nurtured Heart techniques lend themselves to the expression of the love in your heart and the beautiful acknowledgments you want to share.

Your Greatness Unfolding

If you've come this far and practiced these techniques, you've been applying your own brilliance to seeing, describing, and crediting the child's greatness for what is happening *right now, in this moment.* You are being mindful *not* about what's already happened, what you think might happen, or what you hope *will* happen, but what *is* transpiring, in this very moment. You have the greatness of presence and mindful compassion, as well as openness to change. You have willingness to do what it takes to be a force for positive transformation in your child's life. You are *being* the qualities of wisdom and healthy power. We applaud you.

There is so much to recognize in each moment if you set your intention toward doing so. Within this small frame of the Now, you can capture whole universes of success.

The Third Stand
ABSOLUTELY CLEAR!
CONSEQUENCES AND LIMIT SETTING

CHAPTER OBJECTIVES

- Gain a thorough understanding of the importance of the Third Stand in creating the proper balance of consequences, refusal to energize negativity and recognition (appreciation and positive relationship).

- Continue to employ the self-reset.

- Begin to work with resetting your child.

- Learn how to discuss this new mode of giving consequences with your child.

Imagine you've thrown your back out.

Your doctor prescribes a brace to provide stability while the injury heals. Eager to feel some supportive relief, you take the brace from its packaging and try to put it on. But you quickly discover that while two sides of the brace are intact – offering snug, stable support as long as you hold them on with your hands – another, third piece is missing. Try as you might, you can't get the full surround of support your back needs to rest, unknot, and heal.

The First and Second Stands, once firmly in place, make up 2/3 of the "bracing" provided by the Nurtured Heart Approach. Those two parts of the Approach can work wonders all by themselves, as you've hopefully seen. Now, it's time to add in the final part of the Approach – the Third Stand. The Approach will lend some support without this Stand, but it won't give the full bracing that will most support the challenging child and help other children to fully flourish. It's all the pieces in concert that do the trick. Once this last piece is in place, the support you experience will be magnified many-fold.

The First Stand is about flipping the energy characteristic of most parent-intense child relationships: *I get more of you when I misbehave* turns *into you've become really boring when I misbehave.*

The Second Stand creates time-in: ongoing, rich experiences of being profoundly seen, eloquently acknowledged, and celebrated for the greatness that's happening when nothing is going wrong.

The Third Stand is the sorely needed limits piece. Answers to all your burning questions about "What do I do when my child breaks a rule?" are folded into this Stand.

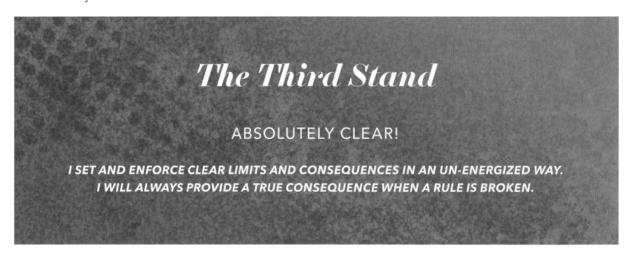

The Third Stand

ABSOLUTELY CLEAR!

I SET AND ENFORCE CLEAR LIMITS AND CONSEQUENCES IN AN UN-ENERGIZED WAY.
I WILL ALWAYS PROVIDE A TRUE CONSEQUENCE WHEN A RULE IS BROKEN.

At the crux of this Stand is the reset. That's right: the time has come to learn to reset others – in particular, your child or children. Pivotal foundational pieces, aside from having the first two Stands up and running, include:

1. **ABILITY TO RESET YOURSELF.** You've already learned about the self-reset in the context of Stand One. Hopefully, by now, you've had multiple opportunities to practice the self-reset in moments where you have been tempted to energize negativity. Hopefully, your child has seen you reset yourself, and perhaps you've had occasion to explain to him or her what you're doing in that moment of radical self-care. As you hold to the First Stand and call up a self-reset of any impulse to participate in negative interaction, we hope you feel supported by impact on your child's subsequent reactivity.

2. **CLEAR RULES, STATED IN THE NEGATIVE.** Setting the stage for effective consequences begins with establishing clear, firm limits and creating time-in when those limits are not being violated. Obviously: you can't enforce limits you have not clearly established! Take time to re-visit your household rules if you see a need. Rules that begin with "no" make it so much more evident when a foot is on the line... and when it isn't. This is likely to be an ongoing process of refinement. If you are highly appreciative when a rule is *not* being broken, negative rules work best to create exquisite clarity.

3. **RIDING THE WAVES OF INTENTION.** Ideally, you've experienced how the intentions of the Nurtured Heart Approach serve you in raising the energies and relationship of Stand Two. Hopefully, you are experiencing how these intentions foster and support you in your creativity and even 'larceny' at times – in terms of stealing opportunities to 'accuse' a child of greatness!

THE RESET IS...

...a pause in engagement from adults that follows the breaking of a rule. The use of the word itself is also a signal to the child that the line has been crossed, the consequence is underway, and the space has been created to eventually say that the consequence has been successfully completed.

It can be as brief as a few seconds. The key is looking for the next moment where a rule isn't being broken, and to build on that. That's precisely what we're fighting for: the truth of the moment that follows a broken rule as closely as possible with a new opportunity for building a growing sense of successfulness in relation to the rules.

This is a time-out in the purest sense, just like the video game time-out: a momentary pause preceding a leap back to time-in. It entails shifting energy back to success. It means nurturing the hearts of everyone involved in the situation by way of the truth of subsequent moments when the rule is no longer being broken. It means recognizing the beauty of that choice: after all, the rule-breaking could continue! How not-great would that be? So, then: how great are the moments when this isn't happening?

...a true consequence. Consider all the tactics adults use as consequences: grounding, removal of privileges, lectures, or having the child go to her room. These are all, fundamentally, time-outs. The child is removed from relationship, fun, and positive recognition – the vibrant time-in. The reset is a purer form of time-out; and just as in the very short reset of the video game, the child will perceive and feel a reset fully as a consequence. When the reset is done cleanly, the child is fully ready to get back into the game in a better-than-ever way. Even two seconds in reset can feel like an eternity when the child can't wait to get back to the greatness of time-in.

HOW TO DO THE RESET WITH YOUR CHILD

To make the reset a truly effective consequence, we have to establish that:

- No more "game in/game on" is available in response to negativity

- A great game in/game on IS available for the child in response to positive choices and for an absence of negative choices

When your child breaks a rule, proceed as follows:

1. Speak a key word like "Reset!" (Feel free to choose a different word with a similar meaning: Pause/Play can work, too, or Stop/Go). You can add "Oops! Broke a rule!" or a similar statement, but be careful to drain all connection and energy from that statement: make it neutral – a statement of fact without judgment.

2. Unplug your energy from the child, briefly. Turn away – not in an emotional or angry way, but in a way that expresses that you are entirely unavailable for connection around the rule that has just been broken.

3. Give no explanation of why the reset is happening or even what rule has been broken. The child will know. And if the child is really unsure about what rule has been broken, he/she will know as soon as the rule-breaking stops and the welcoming-back from reset commences.

4. Remain vigilant in perceiving the truth of the next moments, when the rule is no longer being broken. Be poised to recognize the opportunity for next round of successes to acknowledge.

5. As soon as possible, declare the reset successfully completed and re-connect powerfully with the child around success: "Right now, you aren't swearing at me, even though you're still angry. Thanks for resetting and having such great self-control." This renewal of time-in can happen within seconds of the reset being given.

6. ReNEW: this refers to a very purposeful stance to further the work of Stand Two. It's a reference to going beyond a simple return to the status quo – which is what most time-outs strive to do – and to, instead, with great intention, strive to have even *more* positive impact through next rounds of appreciation, recognition and acknowledgments of greatness.

This reset is a break from connection, interaction, and relationship that will last no longer than a couple of minutes but can be over in two seconds flat. Hold an image in your mind of pulling the plug on energized connection; then, imagine purposefully plugging it in again – renewing connection at ever greater levels – in the moments that follow the reset.

Always keep in mind: this consequence's power comes from its foundation in the first two Stands. There is always room for making both stands more clear, with increasing impact.

The reset is, in essence, a "time-out" – but not the traditional kind, where a child is made to sit in a chair for a number of minutes or to go to a certain part of the room. Any traditional consequence, time-outs included, is about a child's point of view that he is missing out on something desirable.

Whether we send a child to the corner, make her write fifty times that she won't be mean to her sister, or remove screen time or time with friends, we are enacting a time-out. Virtually every consequence we can think of is perceived by the child as a time-out: for the time being, she's out of the loop. Life's opportunities are temporarily unavailable.

The reasons why most forms of time-out don't work are two-fold: When any kind of time-out is paired with the energy of relationship with the parent – lectures, warnings, sympathy, mediation, reprimands, explanations, emotions – it will perpetuate the child's impression that rule breaking is a fast track to connection that might not be available any other way. And when the field hasn't been set up for success via positive connections around what's going well and what isn't going wrong (Stand Two), this *upside-down* impression of getting more out of life through negativity will sink in even more deeply.

Remember the video game – its ideal combination of constant positive feedback, strict rules, and minimally energized consequences. For the child playing that game, even a few seconds' time-out can feel like an eternity. That's what we want: for the reset to feel like missing out on all the fun.

"Really? My kid breaks a rule, and I'm supposed to just give some little reset that lasts a few seconds? And that's going to be an effective consequence?"

Yes. As you learn and practice, you'll see how powerful this simplicity can be. For now, jot down any questions coming up for you around the reset as you consider integrating it into your parenting toolbox. By the time we wrap up this chapter, chances are good that you will be able to answer them yourself.

WE'RE NOT JUST TRYING TO PUT OUT THE FIRE; WE'RE TRYING TO START A NEW FIRE.
We are setting out to transform the very intensity that used to go awry into the new source of fuel for greatness. So those moments when the problem stops, even if they are brief, are the very moments we want to take advantage of – the moments we want to cleave to and build upon.

When you are frustrated with your child, the old you is likely to want to come down hard with a punishment, a removal of a privilege, or something even more drastic. But the truly transformative paradigm comes with seeing the truth of those moments when the problem isn't happening, and pouring yourself into those moments.

THE MOST AMAZING TOASTER ON THE PLANET

Howie stood in the kitchen of a family he was coaching in using this approach. The parents were struggling to understand and correctly use the reset. While casting about for some new way to explain it, Howie noticed the family's gleaming, fancy, multi-feature toaster.

"Let's say this is the most amazing toaster on the planet," he said, indicating the one on the counter. "It toasts everything perfectly, exactly the way you like it. It's intuitive; it knows how you like your toast and when you are going to want it. It butters this perfectly toasted toast to perfection. Let's say it even makes perfect bread on demand."

"Okay…" said the parents.

"Not only can it do all that, it grinds your beans and brews the best coffee, right around the time you get up, just the way you love it, every time. It plays your radio station and knows to switch the channel when a song comes on that you don't like, along with lots of other unique and innovative features. It is truly the best toaster ever."

"That *does* sound like the most amazing toaster on the planet!" said one of the parents. The other nodded in agreement.

"And when you unplug that toaster from the outlet, what happens?" Howie asked.

"The toaster doesn't work."

Right! Plug the toaster back in, it works again; unplug the toaster, its features are inaccessible. Unplugging always gets the same boring result. Plug it in again and you have access to all the bells and whistles. You don't lose one feature or have your favorite features blocked because you unplugged it. It's still the best toaster ever; it simply doesn't work when it's not plugged in.

Resetting a child is like unplugging the world's most amazing toaster. That's how it feels: the thing itself is there, as present as it ever was, but the energy is gone. You still love your child dearly, but that love simply isn't currently flowing. The features don't work until it's plugged in again. Your unconditional love for your child remains whether you're plugged in or not, but the 'gift of *you*' becomes unavailable for the time being. *Access denied. No backstage pass.*

If this feels cold, consider that the same is true when you are asleep. Your child understands that a sleeping parent is as full of love for him or her as an awake parent – but that this love won't be conveyed while that parent is in dreamland.

Not every child will give up easily on re-invigorating relationship around negativity. The more intense the child, the more testing is likely to happen in an attempt to re-engage adults through negativity. This next story will help you see the way through a challenging child's resistance to resetting in particular and Stand Three in general.

THE $2 PARKING TICKET*

Greater intensity often equals a stronger adrenaline rush when pushing boundaries. It stands to reason that risky behavior would be strongly correlated with higher intensity. Do you know someone who often pushes limits? Are *you* that person?

Imagine parking in a convenient spot that you are accustomed to parking in. After your usual errand you return to your car to find an envelope tucked under your windshield wiper. "Have a nice day" is all you see, in neat handwriting. You get into your car and open the envelope. It's a ticket! Angrily, you look around, and only then do you notice that the policy on this street has changed. The part of the street where parking is free and unlimited is now located across the street and one block further away.

Already preparing your argument against the city when you go to contest this ticket, you look back down at it…and notice that the amount you have to pay is only $2.

Relieved, you toss the ticket into your glove compartment and go on your merry way. $2 isn't too much to pay to park in your favorite spot…right?

You return to the same neighborhood on a different day, and you park in your usual spot. You aren't surprised to find another ticket on your windshield. You know what to expect. You don't try to get out of it. "Have a nice day," the envelope says, and you pop the $2 ticket in with the first one and get to your next appointment almost on time.

The next time, you start to feel annoyed. You look around, trying to identify and confront whoever keeps ticketing you, but you never can seem to catch them in the act. Isn't there anyone with whom you can argue, cajole, flirt, flatter, and plead? As someone who has parked here for years without being bothered, can't you be grandfathered in somehow—awarded an honorary free spot? There must be someone you can talk to about this.

All your internal protestations notwithstanding, every time you park in this spot, you find an envelope with "Have a nice day" written neatly on the outside and a $2 parking ticket inside.

Now your ire has been raised. No one's going to stop you from parking wherever you want to park. And every time you return to your car when it's parked there, the same friendly envelope with the $2 parking ticket is there to greet you. There is nobody to hear your reasons, logical debates, or excuses. By now, you have a glove box full of $2 tickets.

A less intense person would have long since gone to plan B: either parked in the free lot down the block or chosen a different street or neighborhood in which to do their business. But that's not you. You have a point to prove. A different plan B. If you have greater intensity, you don't turn over a new leaf that easily. You need to push the boundary, find an exception to the rule. Some even might experience this situation as a call to battle: *game on!* You want a chance to try new antics, excuses, and pleas for mercy to make the story go a different way. Here, however, no matter what you try, every darn time, that same boring "Have a nice day" envelope with its boring $2 ticket awaits you when you park in that spot.

And then, finally, frustration and anger give way to the realization that things have changed, and that this change is beyond your control. Even if you are the world's most intense driver, you will eventually decide, "I'm not doing this anymore." Once you try parking in the designated free lot, and always checking signs around street parking to ensure that you are in a spot where you won't be ticketed, you start to feel how good it feels to be intense around *getting it right*. That's where you begin to put your intensity.

The most intense children - the ones who will benefit most from this transformation - are often the ones who push, test, and twist in the wind the most. The reset is a way for adults to get out of the way and let children like these have a pure experience of this consequence. Some people take longer than others to stop trying to cheat the system. Some kids need to go to the other "plan B."

The $2 parking ticket is the reset. It's not a lot of money. It might not feel like much of a consequence at first. But when it happens repeatedly, hanging you up when you're in a hurry; and when all you get is a neatly written "Have a nice day," with no discussion of fairness or logic of the consequence - it starts to feel like a drag. It becomes boring. And, perhaps more importantly, you come to perceive the reality that this is now the inescapable truth of how things are. *The emotions of frustration and anger ultimately lead the child to her own inevitable solution: to change the behavior that keeps limiting her time in time-in.* We simply need to get out of the way, and - like the parking attendant who always manages to avoid being seen or confronted by the driver who is receiving all these tickets - establish an unplugged and unceremonious way of issuing the consequence.

The child experiences that his or her intensity feels ill-used in the task of breaking rules. One of our deepest needs is to use intensity well. And so, the child shifts. The child comes to see, over time and consistent maintenance of Stands One and Two, that negativity removes her from the loop of connection, and that the 'game in/game on' of energized relationship is now only accessed when rules aren't being broken. Your job, as the parent, is to stay with the Stands, give a calm, un-energized reset every time a rule is broken, and stay out of the child's way as he tests the system.

Getting in the way looks like arguing, responding to the child's pleas, or engaging in "CSI" (Crime Scene Investigation) conversations about what went wrong, when. Discussions of what could have been done better are also verboten. All contribute to and perpetuate the child's existing impression that more can be gotten out of life through negativity.

Your Greatness Unfolding

Committing to the reset as your primary or only consequence requires a big leap of faith. If you are choosing to barrel down this road of being appreciative instead of energizing negativity; if you are choosing to use the energy of frustration to reset to greatness – you have exercised the greatness of faith. As you create a heightened time-in, you find that now, a short time-out can have impact.

You are putting your faith in something that defies the gravity of conventional and old-world approaches. People in your world might be looking at you as though you are a fool; and yet, you remain steeped in clarity, purposefulness, and your mission to help your child to thrive. We applaud you.

Getting *out* of the way looks like the attitude of the parking attendant writing "Have a nice day" and leaving the envelope with zero ceremony.

The child may need a hundred $2 parking tickets to get with the new program, or he may need ten thousand. Either way, your job is the same. Keep resetting yourself. Refuse to escalate, lecture, cajole, or otherwise push the issue (Stand One). Get out of the way and let the child figure it out for himself. Let him develop the internal motivation to shift. Trust that connection with you, with ever-better positive bandwidth, is his ultimate goal; and that he will eventually choose the path that most reliably yields that connection.

For the intense child, the internal relationship between impulse and control is simply underdeveloped.

Many people who work with difficult children are under the false impression that telling a child, "If you try harder, you can do it!" is encouraging. In reality, this is a very discouraging

statement to a child who is *already* trying harder. It takes so much more effort for a difficult child to modulate his intense impulses and energies. It is deflating to be trying very hard and be told to try harder. Besides, the meta-message the child gets when you tell him to try harder is, "You're not trying hard enough right now."

Just like the brakes of a 10-ton cement truck have to work much harder to stop at 20 m.p.h. than a small car at the same speed, intense, energy-challenged, hyper-needy children have to apply much more effort to gain self-control successfully. Like the cement truck, their control mechanisms ultimately have to evolve at much more powerful levels. We need to purposefully build the additional control by applauding what's already there rather than accidentally delivering deflating messages.

An intense child cannot be assumed to have developed the skills involved in using self-control and being adequately aware of limits. Using self-control and learning to assess how well he or she is doing in relation to the rules at any given time are a function of resolve, confidence, belief in oneself, and the way in which brain pathways have been nurtured, strengthened and organized.

*AS YOU IMPLEMENT RESETS, ENSURE THAT YOUR RULES ARE **ABSOLUTELY CLEAR** - THAT THE LINE IS SOLID AND STRAIGHT BETWEEN RULE FOLLOWED AND RULE BROKEN.*

Pieces of the puzzle are not missing. They simply have not yet come together consistently enough for the child's self-control to be adequate for his or her level of intensity. A predominant reason for this is that, until now, the limits have been far too confusing.

ONE MORE LOOK AT THE RULES

As you implement resets, ensure that your rules are *absolutely clear* – that the line is solid and straight between rule followed and rule broken. When the speed limit is 35 mph, going above 35 mph means you're breaking the rule, whether you're going 70 or 36. A toe on the line is a toe on the line. A little bit of a bad word is a bad word.

But the crucial corollary is that even if it looks like a child is *about* to break a rule, and if they apply restraint and don't, then not only is it not a reset, we need to be there applauding the restraint – which, I think we can all agree, is truly a great quality.

Should you post rules? Should you sit the child down to explain them? You can, but you don't have to. Even a preschool-aged child knows the most important rules already. Most times they break rules, they do so with some unconscious or conscious level of intention – that desire to obtain relationship from people around them. If you do want to post or explain the rules, do so in a context of Proactive Recognition: "Whenever you follow these rules, I'm going to do my best to acknowledge your greatness in making those wise choices! Here are the rules I have in mind."

Your child will soon recognize that rules are *good* in this Nurtured Heart context – no longer the enemy – and the more, the better, because she gets recognized for following them. Once you have the reset underway and your child realizes that it is not punitive, you can create rules on the fly.

Let's say your child grabs a sweet treat off a supermarket shelf and drops it into the cart while you walk through the store. Maybe you haven't had a rule addressing this behavior before because the child has never done this particular thing. Simply reset the child as though that rule has always been there, and positively acknowledge the child for not engaging in the behavior as soon as he stops (no longer placing items in the cart without asking). Try a series of Creative Recognitions to move the child to return the sweet item to the shelf; or replace it yourself and energize the child for not having a meltdown when you do it.

INTRODUCING THE RESET TO YOUR CHILD

With younger children – preschoolers, 1st through 3rd graders – you can just start implementing resets. There is usually no need to explain them. They make sense to young children quickly, especially when the first two stands are already in place.

With older children, some explanation might be needed. "You might have noticed that I am focusing a lot more on what you do well and right than on the things you *do* that break rules. I am really enjoying that, and hope you are too. Now, let's talk about how I'm going to respond when you do break a rule. I'm going to give you a quick 'reset,' a chance for you to make a different, better choice. As soon as I see you doing that, I'm going to go right back to telling you what you're doing well."

You can tell the child that she will no longer have to endure lectures, pep talks, or speeches when rules are broken. Neither will she face punishments or long-term consequences. The consequence will end the moment she has taken a reset. Your job as adult is to help her see, repeatedly, with no escalation on your part, that the only thing that stands between her and success is a brief reset. This is true no matter how many times a reset is necessary.

What If...I don't want to turn away from my child when he/she is struggling?

Picture this: a three-year-old child, home with his dad, wants his mom. Eventually, the child launches into a tantrum that leads him to break the rules in several ways (screaming, throwing things). What should Dad do? Or: a 12-year-old is challenged by homework. She's melting down in frustration and feeling sure she's going to flunk the assignment she is working on. She's in tears and is saying rude, argumentative things to the mom – a breach of the family's No Arguing With Parents rule. What should the parent do?

As the parent in these situations, you may feel torn. You see your child's distress, and you want to comfort him or her and get into a conversation about the problem – which means energizing negativity.

Offering comfort and help to "fix" children's problems in the midst of those problems will lead to poorly timed connections around negativity. It is an empathic, loving impulse that will interfere with the process of resetting; and it will, in actuality, feed the old energetic impression you are striving to change.

Struggle is a reality for every human being in every life stage. Applying the stands of the NHA – which indicate *not* diving into relationship around what's wrong, even where emotional upheaval is happening – will help children develop resilience and tools for self-care. This will prepare them to manage their own struggles in their adult lives. Surely they'll have supportive and loving people to be present with them in hard times, but we want them to be OK without others stepping in to fix their problems.

If you see your child struggling, and he's breaking a rule, reset him. Channel the desire to comfort, soothe, and fix into energizing the child's self-care and emotional management: as soon as you can, verbally acknowledge ways in which he is stopping himself from breaking the rules, managing his emotions, and moving back to a place where he can function and follow the rules. This may initially feel as though it lacks compassion, but it is a formula for teaching a child to be resilient and emotionally intelligent. Instead of coming to the child's rescue, appreciate every aspect of resiliency and emotional intelligence you can see in the moment.

If a suffering child is not rule-breaking, choose to energize the positive aspects you see: for example, emotional expression, vulnerability, not taking her stress out on others, and any other aspects of positive character you wish to nurture.

HOW TO KNOW WHEN A RESET IS COMPLETE

The sign that a reset is complete is that the original rule-breaking behavior is no longer happening. The child has reset to *not* breaking rules. It's truly this simple. She may break a rule in seconds to come, but right now, in this moment, she is *not* breaking a rule. It's time to acknowledge and connect in the truth of the moment.

Looking like she is *thinking* about breaking the rule again is *not* a violation of the rule! This approach recommends strongly taking advantage of exactly this kind of opportunity – the moment where the child seems drawn to rule-break, but hasn't – to applaud her current excellent choice. Planting seeds in the fertile soil of those moments shows your compassion, despite any residual frustrations you may be feeling.

What If...My Child Refuses to Reset?

Howard likes to say that with challenging children, limit setting is where the rubber meets the road. One way this manifests is through a child attempting to avoid or refusing to complete a reset. The way you handle these moments will make or break the impact of the approach with these children. Even as they refuse, relentlessly consider all the ways in which they might actually be resetting anyway!

When a younger child crawls under a table or otherwise takes space in order to avoid a reset, find a creative way to see that choice as the reset you've asked for. "I love how you chose to take a reset under the table," you might say. "Great self-care. Reset is done, and now you aren't breaking our rule about arguing with me - you're handling your emotions well."

- If you reset a teen and she responds with a huffy, attitude-laden turning away, you can treat that as a reset, too. Don't say a word during the huffing and puffing; when the rule is no longer being broken, come back and say, "Thanks for resetting in the moment like that. I can see you're upset with me, and right now, you aren't yelling or cursing at me."

- Even if a door was slammed or space was taken, make it your mission to give the child credit for resetting as soon as the rule is no longer being broken. That, plus appreciation of rules not being broken, creates the space for the child to perceive that he has completed a consequence and is back in the game.

In the face of resistance, lean against the Stands. As long as you keep returning to those intentions, and notching up your first two Stands to meet the child's intensity, you will find your way through.

Create strong, clear boundaries without energizing the problem. When a child is pushing hard to get you to give energy for negativity – seeking out all your most reactive "buttons" – it's hard, constant work to reset yourself. Give yourself plenty of energizing statements with every self-reset. Every step of the way, give yourself strong appreciation for resisting the temptation to be reactive.

Always keep in mind that the reset is, essentially, an *illusion* of a consequence. It pauses the action and sets the stage for renewal. That's what makes this ridiculously simple consequence transformative where other punitive and drastic consequences consistently fail. **Let this understanding give you creative license to make successful resets impossible to avoid.**

Challenge

Think of one or two situations where you can imagine your child refusing a reset. How might your child do this? Flatly refusing with a big stomp of her feet? Arguing the wrongness of your call? Throwing a tantrum? Leaving the house? Rule-breaking with ever-greater conviction that she'll get what she wants in return?

Write them down with some space left between them or discuss with a fellow NHA practitioner.

Write or describe a creative way you could translate that resistance into a reset, and how you might subsequently express to the child that she has successfully completed her reset without falling into the trap of reacting to negativity.

CHAPTER 6

WHAT ABOUT SERIOUS INFRACTIONS?

Parents often don't see how these little reset moments could be effective or reasonable consequences for cussing, swearing and defiance, let alone more extreme rule-breaking behaviors like hitting, stealing, self-harm, reckless risk-taking, setting fires, destruction of property, or drug use. We understand this, and it is an important point to address.

At every training, at least one parent, treatment professional, or educator asks, "So you're saying that if a kid hits someone else's kid, I give a 10-second reset?" The answer, which has prompted probably a thousand self-resets, is "yes."

That being said, safety is always top priority. If a child is endangering herself or others, do what you must to get the situation under control, but do it as unceremoniously as possible. Continue to apply Nurtured Heart principles the best you can in those situations. Give the misbehavior as little energy as possible. Avoid lengthy lectures or diatribes. Avoid digging into the problem. Any time rules are not actively being broken, seek ways to energize the child for what is going well.

In receiving harsher consequences for hitting, it's evident to the child that the more serious the infraction, the more energized adults become. This will lead to further testing around energy for negativity.

Our goal is not to squash individual infractions; it is to remove the child's impression that he gets more out of life through the energetics of negative choices. Acting out greatness will follow the change in attunement. The overarching goal is transformation – a goal that far exceeds the temporary improvement that more punitive consequences can bring.

Also, the reset happens in the context of a rich time-in and a refusal to energize negativity – that's not exactly the parent taking the easy way out. This may be hard to explain to an incensed parent of a child who has been hit and who wants to see a severe consequence levied on the hitter, but ultimately, if it is the most effective way to change the unwanted behavior, it's the route most beneficial to all involved. Our experiences have proved this over and over again with some of the most difficult, aggressive, defiant children and young adults imaginable.

Play hardball not through imposing increasingly punitive consequences, but by getting great at Stands One and Two and learning to reset in a blink of an eye. And remember that the real power comes from resetting to the words of appreciation that follow, in response to the new truth of the moment: "Justin, I truly appreciate that you are now not being aggressive with you friends. Thank you for resetting and thank you for showing me the greatness of your power and wisdom to use restraint when you are tempted to lash out. Right now you are being kind, and that shows me your integrity and compassion."

Implementing the Nurtured Heart Approach means choosing to no longer feed the old energetic impression and to take the true warrior route of teaching crucial lessons *when the rule is no longer being broken.*

Consider This ...

If your child has a serious infraction, something more than a reset may be called for. Establish a community service job beyond usual chores that the child is expected to complete to make restitution - something the child can complete with as little guidance as possible.

If you decide that reparations via community service are called for:

1. *Make sure you broach the topic after the reset is complete, and after you've already gotten back to appreciation for next rounds of good choices following the incident.*

2. *Let a bit of time go by so that the child won't feel that he is accessing discussion and relationship through the negativity of the incident.*

3. *Start with appreciation that he has reset; emphasize that right now, the problem that existed before isn't a problem any longer.*

4. *Then, ask for the child's suggestions about suitable reparations. They will often suggest more than you would.*

The very intense child is likely to challenge the approach. This child wants to know, in every setting: "Will the adults here support my success with more energy and engagement than I can get for breaking rules?" To answer this question, the child may go on to test the system with great determination – including acting out more to try to re-establish the old dynamic with which she is most comfortable. If this happens, "notch up" all three Stands (no energy to negativity, relentless positivity, clear and consistent limits) and ride it out. (Much more will be said about 'notching it up' in Chapter Seven.) For the most intense children, a month may be required to get to the turnaround you desire.

CHAPTER 6

What If...I want to take away access to electronic devices or other privileges as a back-up consequence?

Many parents learning the NHA want the option to restrict access to electronic devices as a consequence, in addition to using resets. Although the threat of losing access to electronics is, for most children, a compelling motivation away from rule breaking, we strongly advise against this. It can be a recipe for negativity leaks and energized escalation – an energetic cat-and-mouse game – for the really defiant child.

Taking away screen time in addition to resets muddies the waters instead of creating a squeakier-cleaner Stand Three. If a child needs to be reset, she can be reset even while on a device.

We advise against taking anything away from the child as a consequence for rule breaking. This removal of privileges can bring with it a flavor of guilt or shame that will work at odds with the Stands.

This being said: safety always comes first. If a child is being careless or dangerous with electronics – using them to watch or listen to harmful media, staying up too late using them, or using them to communicate in ways that are destructive to self or others – it may be necessary to remove or restrict access to those items to keep the child safe. If this is necessary, do so with as little energy as possible.

Using removal of screen privileges as a consequence for bad behavior unrelated to screens suggests that those privileges are the gift. Remember: YOU are the gift. Adults often hugely underestimate the impact on the child of "missing out" on their connected energy, even for a few brief moments of resetting. They come to believe they need a crutch, a back-up, something they can take away to enforce a consequence.

Our profound wish: for all youth to develop the ability to reset in the midst of the whole wild world just as it is, replete with distractions and electronics. Removing parts of a child's world in order to foster the reset might work as a short-term solution, but it does not teach the child the vital lesson of self-restraint in the midst of life as it is.

Perhaps you'll decide, still, to try removing a device from the child to help you enact a reset. Maybe you'll have ideas about how to do this cleanly and without energizing negativity. Go for it. If you do decide to go this route, watch the energy keenly. Notice whether, despite all your efforts to the contrary, the child picks up that he/she is getting YOU in response to negativity. Stay tuned to whether the child perceives you as empowered or lacking power.

Any amount of gas on the fire is gas on the fire. Even a tiny ember can blow out into a huge blaze. Watch; notice. See whether it is worth it in the long run.

CONSEQUENCES FOR ATTITUDE?

Yes – teens and tweens who are intense and challenging are masterful at throwing bad attitude. Some parents find themselves on the receiving end of tirades from teens whose anger has gotten the best of them. Although you might decide to have a "no attitude" or "no disrespect" rule, enforced by the reset, to try to move the child in another direction, consider not doing so, at least while you get the approach up and running.

If you can manage to not respond to the eye-rolling, snarky delivery – only to the content of the child's statements, with a constant eye to what's going well – your child will soon recognize that she can't "get" YOU that way. Appreciating her reset after the wave of attitude has passed is a great way to provide closure and create space for increasingly positive interactions.

SAVE YOUR SOUL

One reason resets may not work right away: the parent may be unwittingly undermining his or her commitment to Stand One by giving energy to negativity. Even when this movement of energy is subtle, it reads to the child as an affirmation that the old dynamic is still available. The $100 bills for broken rules can flow in very subtle ways indeed!

Howard likes to share the story of a coaching session with two bright, loving parents and their intense, defiant son. The couple had been using the approach with this 18-year-old young man for a while, and they were underwhelmed with its impact. These parents loved to try to motivate their son with inspired thoughts on how he could solve his problems and make better decisions. Howard watched them interact and saw where they were inadvertently giving the energetic gift of themselves in many instances when the child was under-functioning. He had come to perceive that his procrastination and obtuse choices would lead them to lean in with their loving intention and energy. Where they thought they were interacting in accordance with the Three Stands, they were actually allowing an undercurrent of negativity to undermine the interaction. Instead of giving resets when lines were crossed, they were inadvertently giving the gift of themselves. When that came to a halt, everything quickly changed for the better.

Challenge

Be on the lookout for 'leaks' of negativity. Make a note of them or share about them with a loved one – including whatever you did to reset from those leaks.

Howard directed the parents to speak to him as though he were their son. Whenever their words were purely positive and not energizing negativity in even subtle ways, he moved physically closer to them, even clambering up onto the table where they were sitting to get more connected. As soon as they began to talk in a way that confused the energetic balance and gave even a hint of relationship around something negative, he backed away. There was plenty of laughter in the room, but the parents felt it as a profound illustration of the way energy runs the show in relationships – and how even subtle leaks can create a temporary flip back to a dynamic we don't want. *Save your soul* for all that is good and great, and when that shows up, give of yourself generously. Steadfastly refuse to give even a shadow of your soul, an ounce of your being, or a calorie of your energy, the true gift of *YOU*, to negativity.

A FEW COMMON WAYS WE ACCIDENTALLY ENERGIZE NEGATIVITY

Here are some of the ways in which parents tend to "leak" negativity, undermining Stand One and disrupting the effectiveness of resets:

WARNINGS. Many parents believe it's more compassionate to warn a child first that a consequence is coming. "If you don't _____, then I'll have to reset you!" or "If you _____, that's a reset!" This muddies the line between rules followed/rules broken and confuses the child about whether the reset is a true consequence. Ultimately, the most compassionate route is to let go of warnings entirely. Either the rule has been broken or it hasn't. If it has, what is needed is a simple reset and return to success.

PEP TALKS. "I just know you can follow this rule! I've seen you do it before!" Or how about, "You've got everything you need to do better right now. Just go for it!" Anything resembling a pep talk carries this energetic subtext: "I know you *could* be successful right now, but you aren't." NHA recognitions come only in response to successes in the current moment or in the past. Referring to a hoped-for success in the future is not in alignment with the approach. It implies failure and is a leak of negativity.

LECTURES ABOUT BROKEN RULES. It can be almost impossibly tempting to lecture a child when she is coming back from a reset: "Do you know what you did wrong? Do you know why I reset you?" Reset yourself away from that impulse. Only lecture the child about rules being followed. That's right – positive lectures only!

'CRIME SCENE INVESTIGATIONS' (CSIs). Any variation on exploring the question of why a child chose to break a rule constitutes a leak of negativity. Don't go there!

EMOTIONALITY AROUND GIVING RESETS. Giving a reset from anything but a totally neutral stance will energize negativity. Don't let yourself express anger, regret or sadness around resetting a child: no "That's it…you've really done it now…that's a reset!" and no "I'm sorry, but I have to reset you for that broken rule." Rather, maintain the greatest possible neutrality around resets, resetting *yourself* where needed. Avoid consoling a child who is in reset, even subtly (a pat on the back, an empathic look). Even a well-intentioned hug following a reset could be energetically interpreted as relationship obtained via the original broken rule.

GIVING A RECOGNITION IN TANDEM WITH A PEP TALK, A WARNING, OR A LECTURE. Keep recognitions clear and clean, without a tinge of negativity. "Here's how you are being successful, BUT…" will always backfire.

SARCASM IN ANY FORM. Sarcasm is defined as "the use of irony to mock or convey contempt." Obviously, neither contempt nor mockery aligns with this approach. If you are someone who enjoys sarcastic humor, we're sorry to say that it has no place here, and will undermine your efforts to shift the dynamic with your child. Notice your tendency toward sarcasm and actively work to move any remaining trace of it out of your interactions with your child.

ACKNOWLEDGING OTHER CHILDREN WITH THE INTENTION OF SHAMING THE CHILD WHOSE BEHAVIOR CALLS FOR A RESET. We've seen educators avoid calling a needed reset with one student by complimenting other children, with an undercurrent of "See how well these *other* students are doing?"

Here's the truth: *everybody* who uses this approach will accidentally give the gift of who he/she is at the wrong time. Keeping the approach squeaky-clean is a laudable aim, but know that everyone slips up and accidentally energizes negativity. When you catch yourself doing this, reset and acknowledge your own resiliency, self-understanding, perceptivity and inner strength in continuing to practice and refine the approach for the good of your child and yourself. Knowing this, give yourself a ton of credit when you don't give energy to negativity, especially when it's tempting and you reset yourself.

> *EVERYBODY ACCIDENTALLY ENERGIZES NEGATIVITY! WHEN YOU CATCH YOURSELF, RESET AND ACKNOWLEDGE YOUR NEXT MOMENT OF SUCCESS. CALL OUT THE QUALITIES OF GREATNESS INHERENT IN YOUR ONGOING WORK WITH THE NHA.*

The gifts of YOU – the energy of discussion, explanation, connection and relationship in the midst of negativity – are the single greatest reason why traditional time-outs do not work. They create consequences that are confusing mixed messages. Sometimes, old forms of time-out even come gift-wrapped with lengthy mediation sessions about how things can be improved next time. The child still connects the dots by perceiving that he gets the gift of you by way of problems.

Teach all the lessons you hold in your heart, but do it through recognition of the beauty of your child not having the problem. Go into lengthy explanations, as long as you are detailing the benefits of all the qualities and choices of the child that make the problem *not a problem*. Then, you can say all you've ever wanted to say in a way that will be positive and fully heard. You'll be able to deliver your message without the child defending against it.

Challenge

Begin practicing resets with your child. Do them often, and let it be fun – goofy, even – to help shift the notion of punishment into an on-the-ground sense that resets are not bad; they are not punishments; they are simply opportunities to make a different choice more aligned with the rules. Make it your mission to demonstrate the truth of that new reality.

Try for 15-30 resets in a day. Continue to reset yourself, too, as needed.

SUMMING UP STAND THREE

Remember: if resets aren't working, attend to one or both of these factors:

1. Strive to get better and better at not giving energy to negativity

2. Strive to get greater and greater at creating a sufficiently strong field of energy, appreciation and connected relationship when rules are not being broken

In other words:

JUICY, NURTURING TIME-IN = SUCCESSFUL TIME-OUTS.
The real beauty and power of Stand Three and the reset become evident as children begin to take ownership of the value of limits and resets. They internalize the process and need fewer and fewer resets. Eventually, they learn to fully reset themselves. Learning to reset paves a fast-track to resiliency – the quality of greatness that characterizes the world's creative geniuses, risk-takers, adventurers, innovators and contributors to the collective greatness.

The reset helps create an impression of the world not as a place full of risk and danger of failure, but as a place where success and positivity are only ever a reset away.

Notching It Up

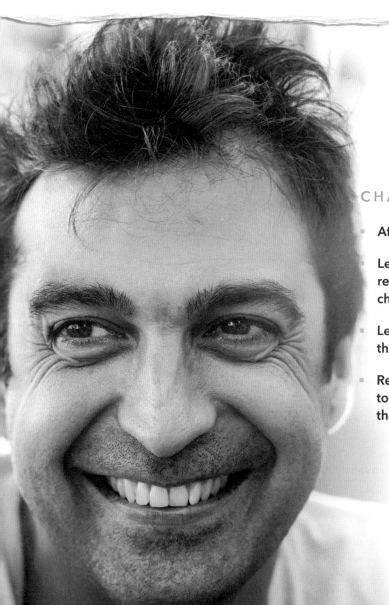

CHAPTER OBJECTIVES

- Affirm the NHA as a "warrior path."

- Learn how to "notch up" the approach in the face of resistance, and why this is the way through to the most challenging children.

- Learn why it might be harder for some people to self-reset than others.

- Reinforce your understanding of the Three Stands and how to make them all cleaner, clearer, and more effective when the going gets rough.

CHAPTER 7

The Nurtured Heart Approach is about the art of making the most of the moment.

At first glance, thanks to its name and its emphasis on positivity, some figure it to be gentle, sweet, or lenient. We hope that by now, you recognize that this approach isn't any of these things: that it is, in fact, a warrior path.

The dictionary defines a warrior as someone who specializes in combat or warfare. It can also describe someone who shows great vigor or courage, or who (in the case of a "spiritual warrior") battles ignorance or seeks self-discovery.

In the NHA context, warriorship is about passionately adopting a set of intentions. It means strengthened commitment and follow-through in the face of challenge and resistance. Nurtured Heart warriorship is about *notching it up* within the framework of the approach's stands and intentions.

Traditional approaches to discipline get more punitive as children get more challenging. Any adult who has been faced with a child whose circumstances have created out-of-the-park intensity knows how this generally goes. It becomes a battle of wills. It takes over the relationship; the family; the classroom. Most approaches wind up falling apart at the seams when this happens.

We live in a world where we inadvertently give great recognition when things are going wrong. When the going gets rough, we tend to give the gift of ourselves reflexively and with growing intensity through ever-stronger reprimands, lectures, or punishments. By now, you may realize that any energy, even energies that flow when things go wrong, are inadvertently perceived by the other as love.

You are in the process of converting to a full-on version of loving congruently, while disengaging any old remnants that might support the child's belief that she can still gain access in unaligned and negative ways. Now is the time to pull out all the stops and take this new approach to any level needed to serve the children that brought you to this process.

No matter what the child throws at you, hold on to the Three Stands as though your life depended on them. Reset yourself as many times as necessary. As you reset and renew, pour all the energy of frustration and challenge into making these Stands squeakier-cleaner than ever before.

Rather than relenting on your Stands and giving energy to negativity when the going gets tough; rather than pulling the plug on the positives when the going gets tougher – turn up the dial. You now are not only standing your ground, you may be taking the approach to levels you never thought were possible.

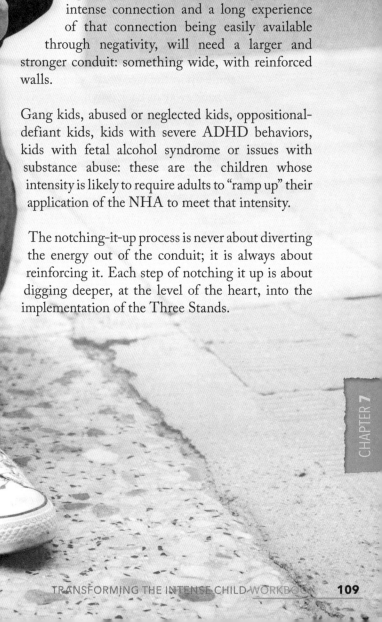

Think of the approach as a conduit that holds and appropriately channels relationship energy between adult and child. Some relationships will only require a smallish conduit with thin walls to hold the energy they need. Others, especially those where there is high need for intense connection and a long experience of that connection being easily available through negativity, will need a larger and stronger conduit: something wide, with reinforced walls.

Gang kids, abused or neglected kids, oppositional-defiant kids, kids with severe ADHD behaviors, kids with fetal alcohol syndrome or issues with substance abuse: these are the children whose intensity is likely to require adults to "ramp up" their application of the NHA to meet that intensity.

The notching-it-up process is never about diverting the energy out of the conduit; it is always about reinforcing it. Each step of notching it up is about digging deeper, at the level of the heart, into the implementation of the Three Stands.

The general rule: When faced with resistance, make your Stands squeakier-cleaner. Each NO becomes clearer and more powerful, as does each YES. Rules and limits, too, become clearer. The overall clarity of life becomes ever more great.

Notch the application of the approach up to whatever level is needed to convince the child that the rules of the game have changed. It is this YES energy of greatness that ultimately wins the day. Space for this is created as Stand One and Stand Three become solid and consistent. As your appreciation lands without interference, its trajectory becomes the pervasive bandwidth that carries your messages of recognition deeply into the child's being.

Notice how your own worries, misery and doubts (WMDs), fears, frustrations, resistance or resentments come up in the face of the child's resistance. Reset to an ever-deeper conviction that resistance is not a cue to back away or back down, but is instead a signal to get clearer and cleaner about your intentions and with your application of the approach. Let your energy meet the child's energy with equal intensity while holding to the Stands as though your life depended on them.

Enter this cycle through the top heart (the one radiating red) as you meet resistance or experience frustration. Take a breath, dial in the three stands, and continue around the circle. The situation may resolve itself at any point in that cycle. It could happen right away, or you might need to go around the loop several times. Stay present to each step along the way as you notch it up.

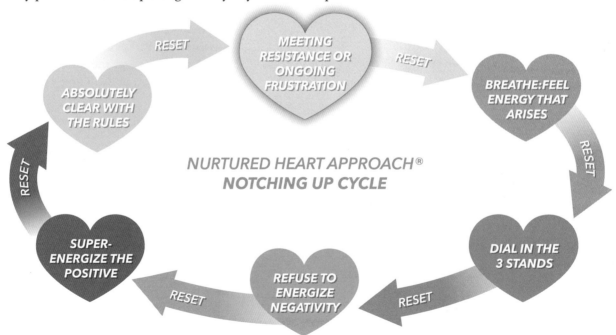

CHAPTER 7

Emphasize getting "squeakier-cleaner" around refusal to give energy to negativity. There's almost always room to create ever-stronger versions of this as we begin to develop "x-ray vision" to detect where the child continues to perceive or push for connection through negativity. That is where we stay most present to the need to reset: to pull the plug on the energies and gifts of ourselves.

Notch it up by resetting to super-energizing the positive while staying absolutely clear with the rules. Breathe into any energy that arises at any point; use it as jet fuel to dial into the three Stands. Again, there are almost always next levels of becoming more present to the truth of the moments where problems are not happening – and where great choices are unfolding.

What If...I'm afraid of my child breaking the rules?

Many adults have a strong emotional charge around rules being followed. Often, this has to do with the adults' own childhood experiences or the way they've parented up until they discovered the NHA. If this fear comes up, really engage the self-reset. See it as an invitation to notch it up.

If your challenging child recognizes that he can get your goat by breaking rules or threatening to break them, you are over an energetic barrel. This is a common underlying thread of negativity for many adults who implement the NHA.

Children who recognize that they can break the rules, reset, renew, and step back into their greatness are developing strength that will serve them for their entire lifetimes. The best way to do this is to show the child that your goat doesn't live here anymore, so to speak. As children test and have new core experiences where there is no longer a goat to be gotten, they begin to take a new course. They are free to discover for themselves the new runway of positivity that you've been widening, paving, and lighting up.

You can see rule-breaking as something to be avoided or feared, or you can see it as an opportunity for these kinds of exploration and growth. Feel the energy of fear. Feel the energy of anger and frustration whenever that comes up for you. Move it into the next moments of success. Move it to fire up greater than ever levels of intention. Move it to motivate you to ever-greater levels of clarity. Fear has powerful energy that can serve as fuel for digging in and finding your way to next levels of all three Stands. Every step of notching up claimed and achieved will result in movement forward for your child.

Every single aspect of this approach can be strengthened, and this just might be necessary. Some kids need to throw the kitchen sink at you. Some kids are lost and craving to be found. They might fight you every step of the way – until they realize they're being seen in their greatness, and that this is what they've wanted all along.

These kids have always had relationship through negativity – they've had it since before they could talk.

Some may crave congruent relationship, but they aren't going to make it easy on you. But when you get there, you will know they've been calling you to rise to this occasion all along. We're willing to bet you will feel great about all you've inspired in this child. It will seem to you as if the greatness was there all along, just waiting for the proper channels to open up and allow it to flourish. You are the one calling it up and ushering it in, making this impact possible by all you are doing and the inroads you are creating.

Some kids are designed to test you with all they have, to see if you're for real. Are you going to dive in as far as needed and go for transformative relationship, persistently and appreciatively expressing what's going great, or are you just going to control and manage them – show up intermittently to right the ship, then fall asleep again?

If you persevere, if you really notch it up as often and as intensely as necessary for as long as it takes, this approach will work its magic on even the toughest kids. At this level, it's not for the faint of heart; it's for playing hardball.

Notching it up is breathing, resetting, and reNEWing the Stands: refusing to return to the status quo, but striving toward greatness. It is not NHA plus other forms of leverage. It is not departing from the Stands, but using and repeating them at ever-deepening levels.

Notching up is about trusting that your heart's full voice knows best what to do and say, and that this is what will lead you toward more impact and authenticity. After all: it's not the Nurtured Head Approach.

Notching it up is about trusting that it will work at some next level; that it is a cumulative process with cumulative impact. This impact might not be directly visible in the moment, and this is why trust is so important.

NOTCHING UP THE SELF-RESET

Self-resets are inherent in the approach as a whole, and are especially foundational to the First Stand. If you have made progress with not giving your energy and relationship to negativity, then you are already resetting. If you have deepened your refusal to give energy to negativity, then you are already notching up this pivotal ability to reset.

Your ability to reset to being non-reactive, like the officer in the speed limit story, is essential to your child's acceptance of his new reality. Your commitment to resetting yourself is key to building his ability to fully use his intensity to live in his greatness. The ability to reset yourself becomes even more important when you face deepening resistance in response to notching up the approach.

If you tend to be highly emotional or reactive, your reactions to your child's rule breaking may sometimes threaten to overwhelm your ability to reset yourself. When your child begins to push your buttons, you might feel your heart start to race, your face start to become hot, or other changes in your body consistent with an oncoming fight-or-flight reaction. This is true of all human beings, but may feel more overwhelming for some. Those who have experienced trauma, especially in early childhood, may have a stronger fight-or-flight response. This can make the self-reset more challenging.

It's believed that early adverse life experiences directly affect our thresholds for strong emotions. Current research demonstrates that this has to do with actual changes in the calibration of the fight-or-flight response. If this is true for you, you may be wired to react strongly to negativity, making the self-reset a steeper challenge – especially when resistance is an issue.

If this is true for you, know that we bring it to your attention not to discourage you, but to help you be more forgiving with yourself and not give up on building that "muscle" of refusing to energize negativity. As you continue to practice this, you will 're-wire' your responses to your child's misbehavior. You are, effectively, changing your default settings. Every time you achieve a successful self-reset, you lay new pathways in your brain that improve emotional control and make each subsequent self-reset feel more natural and easeful.

As soon as you realize you're energizing the negative, reset yourself, even if you've gone way, way down the rabbit-hole. Remember that every moment is a new opportunity. We always *eventually* successfully reset, no matter what, so we may as well make that happen sooner than later.

We've seen people who never thought they could be non-reactive become absolute stars of resetting. They learn to pull the plug of energy instantly and beautifully. This is a skill that can be developed even when there is a strong predisposition toward reactivity.

Your Greatness Unfolding

If you are easily triggered and struggle with the self-reset, create support for yourself to facilitate steady practice in this First Stand. And when you know you're overwhelmed or about to be, know you may need to remove yourself from the situation for some intensive self-care (deep breathing, soothing music, a hot bath, a hug, or quality time in a peaceful place) before re-connecting with your child. If the situation allows you to step away to reset yourself, you can tell the child that this is what you're doing, and that you'll be back as soon as you feel calm again. This models the greatness of self-care and of commitment to managing tough emotions.

If you come from a history of any kind of abuse, the work you are doing to gain control over emotional reactivity toward your child is heroic. You are breaking a cycle. There is no greater service you can perform for your child or the world in which she is growing up.

Whether it's hard for you to reset or easy, ultimately, the issue is the same. Eventually, it's going to happen, whether it takes a year, a month, or a minute. You can devote your energy to worrying, telling yourself stories about how hard this is for you and why; or you can devote it to resetting.

Many parents, teachers and treatment professionals get thrown right at the moment of truth: when the intense child is in the dying throes of the old pattern and is pulling out all the stops on testing. This is where the rubber meets the road. Your refusal to divert from the map of notching it up will carry you through to a place where the child can transform. For some, it can't happen without intense testing, but parents often interpret this testing as a sign that the approach isn't working.

When you face testing from a difficult child, remember: where all your challenging feelings surface – from frustration to anguish, from core anger to deep sadness and on into heart-wrenching concern – it is most important for you to remain steadfast in your Stands.

Know that the intensity of the feelings that bubble up here are directly correlated with how deeply you care. You can convert these same challenging emotions into jet fuel for the next steps of notching it up. At this juncture, it's not about "processing" these strong feelings through or making the discomfort go away. Rather, it is about seizing an opportunity to use the enormous storehouse of energy held in these feelings as the pure fuel, intention, impetus, and drive for the next steps of the fight.

Let these raw feelings engage the gears of your warrior nature. Let them support you in launching the approach at higher levels, which is what is often called for when the child takes testing to the hilt.

To convert your primal emotional energy into nutrition for these crucial next steps of Notching Up:

1. Feel the feelings deeply and efficiently. Don't make them bad or try to make them go away. Lovingly thank the emotions, if you can, for the energy they are providing.

2. Deeply breathe in every ounce of energy these big emotions have to offer. Feel where they are located in the body and interpret these sensations as pure energy.

3. Breathe this energy fully into your heart, with a growing trust that your heart can convert this raw energy into the determination, willpower and guidance needed for next steps.

4. Let this energy fuel an ever-greater NO in Stand One and ever-greater resolve to uphold the YES of Stand Two. Let it fuel ever-greater clarity for Stand Three, where a little bit of a broken rule is a broken rule but a foot not quite on the line is not, and where even greater opportunity for appreciation exists. Another way of saying it: the greater the NO gets, the greater the YES becomes; and the clearer the YES becomes, the clearer the NO becomes.

5. Let this energy fuel your warrior nature and the warrior nature of this approach.

6. Breathe this energy into your cause of transformation. It's not a lost cause. It's not a matter of whether you can or can't: you *are*.

NOTCH IT UP TO GREATNESS

When a child refuses resets, don't resort to old punitive consequences: notch it up. If a child acts out more than he did before you enacted the approach: notch it up. If a child says she hates all these compliments and if you don't stop it she's going to really give you something to complain about: notch it up.

Notch it up by:

- Sticking to the truth of the moment.

- Trusting that resistance is a sign that energy is shifting and healing is underway.

- Relentlessly refusing to give energy to negativity.

- Relentlessly confronting success of rules not broken.

- Relentlessly appreciating the goodness and greatness of choices made in the direction of kindness, compassion, thoughtfulness, wisdom, integrity and more.

- Trusting that your heart will give rise to loving words of appreciation.

- Trusting that your heart has both the voice and guidance required to convey the primal nutrition of these words to the child.

- Knowing that your words ultimately empower this child to appreciate her own greatness. Through your acknowledgment, you convey that this child is profoundly seen and appreciated; you trust that her inner wealth is growing.

- Remembering that warnings are not compassionate. The greatest compassion comes through the simplicity of clear limits and simple use of resets when rules are broken.

- Knowing that you are breaking the child's addiction to pushing limits.

- Knowing and conveying that resets are a consequence, but not a punishment.

This is the way through to the relationship you've always wanted with the children in your life. And ultimately, it's the way through to the most nourishing, positive, and life-affirming relationship with yourself.

Extending Success to School

CHAPTER OBJECTIVES

- Recognize the importance of creating a bridge from home to school and back for the challenging child.

- Develop a game plan for meeting with the child's teachers, where they are asked to either explore and implement the Nurtured Heart Approach or fill out a simple note for the child on a regular basis.

- Learn to use the note home to reinforce the child's successes in school and to enact resets for rules broken in school.

- Learn how the NHA has been used effectively to transform classrooms, schools, and districts.

CHAPTER 8

We all hope for our children to do well in school:

to be liked, to get along well with the teacher, to learn all they need to learn in order to prepare for a functional and joyful adulthood, and to enjoy their educational experience. That milestone can become a heavy weight on a parent's shoulders when the news from school isn't good.

"Your child is hard to handle."

"Your child is disruptive."

"Your child doesn't focus or participate."

"Your child is out of control."

"You might want to have your child evaluated."

Teachers are faced with more intense, oppositional, challenging children than ever before. Most teacher education programs fail to prepare them for the challenge of simultaneously teaching curriculum and managing difficult student behavior. Current data show that nearly half of new teachers either transfer to a new school or leave teaching altogether in the first five years. Not surprisingly, schools with more disadvantaged students (as measured by eligibility for free or reduced-price school lunches) have greater turnover.

For many teachers, their decision to leave has to do with the unexpected challenge of reaching students who can't seem to sit still or follow the rules, or who are clearly more interested in resisting and opposing than in learning.[3]

Teachers are not generally given strategies that prepare them for the intense children they are guaranteed to encounter. Most of their professors at schools of education have either never been in a classroom or have been out of the classroom so long that they have no idea of the level of intensity of children in this day and age.

Now that you understand what's behind the acting-out of these students, and now that you've begun to see results in your use of this approach, you may feel eager to share what you've learned with your child's teacher(s). This may feel especially important if your child is doing better at home as a result of your impact, yet is still getting negative reports from school.

WHY IT'S IMPORTANT TO BRIDGE HOME AND SCHOOL

The average child spends six hours or more a day in school. Bridging home and school will enhance the impact of the Approach. Imagine the potential benefit to your child if you successfully enlist your child's educators in your efforts to transform your child through the Nurtured Heart Approach. A teacher who really gets on board will help not only your child, but also all his or her classmates and every student taught from that point forward.

Phillips, Owen, "Revolving Door of Teachers Costs Schools Billions Every Year," http://www.npr.org/sections/ed/2015/03/30/395322012/the-hidden-costs-of-teacher-turnover

Creating the Bridge: Two Options

We'll recommend a two-step approach, moving from the first to the next if the first does not have the desired impact.

1. **Meeting with or writing to your child's teacher(s) about the approach and its impact that you have experienced, and asking for the teacher to help bridge the child's home and school lives via the NHA in a very simple, non-time-consuming way.** In the best-case scenario, the teacher's interest will be piqued, and he or she will want to know more about the approach. Refer him or her to books and trainings to learn more and offer whatever support you feel you can to facilitate the teacher's learning and using the NHA in his or her classroom. It's important not to approach the teacher until you can speak from the experience of your efforts and the results you have seen. Otherwise it will come off as theoretical and philosophical and not carry the experiential weight you intend.

2. **If the teacher refuses to work with you, insist that the child has a right to modifications that are within reason to help him or her do well in school.** This is true whether the child has a formal diagnosis or not. Move up the chain of command to ensure that this will be done. (More on this, too, later on.)

TALKING WITH YOUR CHILD'S TEACHER: A FEW POINTERS

Educators can take so much precious time working up IEPs, creating special classes, putting out fires, and dealing with disciplinary issues. If a teacher has been struggling with your child, and if you are able to clearly convey that you are offering an intervention that will take the teacher less than 30 seconds a day – way less than it takes to repeatedly deal with disruptions – it should be possible to move through even strong resistance.

That being said, not all teachers are open to trying something new. Those who have practiced conventional methods for some time, and for whom those methods work with most children, may be the hardest to persuade.

Let your child's teacher(s) know that you would like to discuss a new approach you have been using successfully with your child; that you would like their participation; and that this participation will only require 30 seconds or so of their time each school day. Arrange to meet or connect by phone, in person, or via e-mail.

Begin the conversation with a brief "elevator speech" describing the approach. For example:

"I have been learning an approach to parenting intense children that has had remarkable impact at home. Basically, it involves not giving energy or relationship around negative choices or rule breaking while giving lots of positive energy and relationship around what the child does right. It involves the parent learning to see successes in any moment where rules are not being broken, while holding the child fully accountable every time a rule is broken through a brief 'reset' that gives the child a chance to make a better choice."

Or, "I'm using the Nurtured Heart Approach at home and [child's name] is responding beautifully there. It's based in three Stands – refusing to energize negativity, committing to energize what's going well as much as possible using detailed, specific appreciations, as well as strictly but non-punitively enforcing the rules. This increases the child's 'inner wealth' and helps her want to make better choices."

Or, "I have been using an approach with my child that is easy to learn and that has helped my child's coping skills and mood regulation. She takes more initiative and can handle more responsibility. It works by not giving energy to negative behaviors and by giving her ongoing experiences of success, which I create through taking three simple stands that are helped along by a few simple techniques and a few key intentions."

Or, even better: speak from your own heart and experience.

NHA Reflection and Action Step

Write two or three variations on the NHA "elevator speech," personalizing it for your own child and the changes you've seen in him or her.

Practice your speeches with your partner or a friend if you plan to meet or speak on the phone with your child's teacher(s).

THE BRIDGING NOTE

Some teachers have their own theories and practices set in stone. Some schools have policies in place that mandate responses to rule-breaking that conflict with the approach you are now using. Even if the latter is the case, you can still have impact on your child's choices at school.

Whether the teacher wants to learn more or not, request that he or she help your child bridge home and school through a very brief checklist that you will supply. Your child will bring these notes to school and give them to the teacher to complete. Daily checklists are best; once or twice a week is OK, but may be harder for the child to remember to bring and hand to the teacher when it isn't a daily routine. The child will be responsible for bringing the completed and signed checklists home; the parents will then make a point of discussing all the successes shown on the list with the child that same day.

CREATING THE BRIDGING NOTE

Two sample checklists are shown below – one for younger children who have one main classroom teacher, and one for older children who may have several teachers. When considering items to include in your child's checklist, be sure to include 'gimme' items with which the child is likely to almost always succeed (Baby Steps) as well as rules or behaviors that are currently creating some level of struggle for the child. Include both positives you want to see and rules you want to see followed. Emphasize with the teacher the importance of giving partial credit wherever possible. Emphasize that it is crucial to have a few listings where success is *highly* likely. Share, too, that perfection is not required for partial credit.

For very young children who are unlikely to be able to remember to give checklists to teachers as scheduled, give a stack of blank checklists to the teacher to fill out and send home. Older children can be counted on (and energized) to give the checklist to their teacher on schedule and to bring it home to you.

Use a scoring method that makes partial credit a possibility in the way each item is scored: a range of "poor" to "excellent" or a scale of 1-5 correlating with this range. We've listed several options for behaviors to recognize; your form can include some, all, or others.

Name of child
Teacher's name
Date

	Poor	Fair	Good	Very Good	Excellent
Completing class work					
Following directions					
Good lunchroom behavior					
Good self-control					
Good responsibility					
Good problem solving					
Sharing					
Paying attention					
Class participation					
No arguing					
No angry outbursts					
No teasing					
No distracting					
Staying in seat					

Comments:

Most children in middle or high school will have multiple teachers. A checklist for a child this age could look like this:

Child's Name:	1st Period	2nd Period	3rd Period	4th Period	5th Period
Responsible choices					
Being respectful					
Classwork completed					
Homework turned in					
Self-restraint					
Rules followed *					
Positive participation					
Comments					
Teacher's Initials					

Scale: 1 - poor; 2- fair; 3 - good; 4 - very good; 5 - excellent

* You can make this general statement – "Rules Followed" – or you can list several specific rules on the sheet.

As you design these checklists for your child's teachers and enroll their support, emphasize:

- That collaborating with you in this way will make her or his job easier by allowing you to acknowledge the child at home for all academic and behavioral efforts made in school.

- That you are open to his or her input as you create the checklist: where does the teacher see areas for prospective growth for the child? Where does the teacher see the child as already successful?

If the teacher is resistant to completing a daily checklist, suggest three times a week or even twice. Mention that as the child progresses within the approach, fewer weekly notes will be needed to maintain the child's positive shifts. Whatever the teacher's response, keep the meeting brief and positive; persuade by describing successes at home; and be welcoming to any feedback the teacher might have. Being strategically appreciative of your child's teacher can ultimately be what creates the openings you are seeking. **In our experience, even when a teacher is resistant, acknowledging his or her deep caring, creative spirit, and deep belief in his or her mission to teach are connecting points that help the heart of both parent and teacher to open.**

If teachers refuse to help with this simple accommodation, check your school's advocacy policies. For most publicly funded schools, a child is entitled to a reasonable accommodation if her behaviors interfere with her own learning or the learning of others, regardless of whether he or she has a formal diagnosis. Asking a teacher to spend 30 seconds with this checklist each day, or on at least one day each week, is quite a reasonable accommodation. Every district has a designated person to help enact steps toward successful accommodation; contact the district office if necessary to put this in motion. It is a requirement that they must enforce if implored to do so.

Explaining the Home-to-School Link to Your Child

Talk to your child about your desire to get more information from school about his successes, especially now that things are so much better at home. **Make clear that you want this in place so that you can *celebrate* those successes.** Give the child a chance to contribute to the checklist any qualities or behaviors she wishes to see recognized or to enhance in herself. Now that you've implemented the stands of this approach your child will much more likely embrace your desire to be further appreciative.

Some parents include a checklist for the teacher(s) and one for the child to fill in, or an extra column where the child can add his own input. This helps the child learn to recognize his own successes in school and to talk about his perception of that success with his parent(s).

REFUELING, RESETTING AND RENEWING: THE MOST IMPORTANT PART OF THE HOME-TO-SCHOOL LINK

These checklists are aimed at two over-arching goals: to build the child's inner wealth and sense of school success and to create a perception for the child that there is accountability that extends from school to home. This happens through the refueling and reNEWing conversation you have with the child once she returns home with the completed checklist after being apart from you for the whole school day.

Intense children will need a renewed connection in greatness with the NHA-practicing adults in her life after a day at school, especially if their school adheres to traditional discipline styles that are meager on stronger versions of appreciation and if the child has been able to receive energetic payoffs for negativity there. Anticipate the need for this renewal by carving out a few minutes as soon as you and the child are back together. If the child isn't able to proactively get positive connection, he or she may revert to a tendency to push for a negative connection.

CHAPTER 8

Pointers for the Refueling Conversation

- *Don't open with questions like "How was your day?" Tell the child, "It's great to see you - let's look at how the day went."*

- *Right away, focus on opportunities to acknowledge and appreciate. Start out by giving appreciations for the child's getting the note filled out and bringing it home.*

- *Then, dive into giving verbal recognition for every degree of success beyond the category of "poor" or rating of "1."*

- *For every score of "1" or "poor," give a reset.*

- *Let each reset be straightforward, simple, brief, unceremonious and sermon-free.*

- *Welcome the child back after every reset and focus on the next success.*

- *Use this time to challenge yourself to explore and appreciatively express further into the successes that are already there, to unfold them further and to see ever more deeply into the efforts and realms of wisdom involved in those successes.*

By letting a rich conversation about the child's successes in school unfold you will see the child's inner wealth grow with each round of recognition.

Check in periodically with the teacher once the notes begin to come home; use any input as further fodder for positive appreciations for the child. Give the teacher all the appreciation you can muster for any movements in the right direction.

Typically, within a week or two, once the energetic alignment of school is bolstered by your efforts at home; once nutritious appreciation is flowing for efforts that may likely have previously gone unnoticed; and once an overarching sense of simple and unceremonious accountability is reached by way of resets at home for school infractions, children we've worked with tend to begin "acting-out" their greatness in school too, regardless of whether the teacher or school has jumped on board with directly using the approach.

Ask the teacher whether he or she is interested in learning the Approach and using it in the classroom. This will help your child thrive by improving consistency from home to school. You may want to bring a copy of this book or the most current book for educators, *Notching Up the Nurtured Heart Approach: The New Inner Wealth Initiative for Educators*, in case the teacher is open to reading it. You can also refer the teacher to the Children's Success Foundation website (**www.childrenssuccessfoundation.com**) and the free e-course resources listed there.

Remain empathic in these conversations. Think back on your own resistance early in learning this approach; think of all the questions you had and all the advice that sounded counterintuitive at first. The Nurtured Heart Approach way of dealing with resistance is to see it as energy that can be worked with; approach resistance from teachers in the same way. Remain grounded in curiosity and appreciation rather than negative judgment: walk the NHA talk!

IN TALKING WITH YOUR CHILD'S TEACHER, WALK THE NHA TALK BY REMAINING GROUNDED IN CURIOSITY, ENERGIZING THE POSITIVE, AND REFRAINING FROM NEGATIVE JUDGMENT OR ENERGY TO NEGATIVITY.

Don't force the larger issue of trying to move the approach into the child's classroom if the teacher seems uninterested. Although it may feel frustrating to you when you feel that a teacher who struggles with difficult children is only lacking the right approach, remember that sometimes people don't "get it" until they have had exposure to the results.

That being said, you are entitled to approach every interaction with your child's teacher(s) through a Nurtured Heart lens. Request a focus on successes in parent-teacher conferences. Frequently appreciate the teacher(s) for their successes, too.

CHAPTER 8

NHA IN SCHOOLS: THE BIG PICTURE

Educators in the U.S. and overseas are implementing the NHA with great success. We hear many happy stories of students, classrooms and schools transformed. As a movement, the NHA contingency aims to create Nurtured Heart classrooms, schools and school districts. Our Certification Intensive Trainings (CTIs) nationwide and worldwide are largely populated by educators and therapists who hold this vision as a way of positively transforming schools and communities. Parents attending to learn the approach for their own parenting purposes have also had transformative impact in bringing the approach to their world and beyond.

A growing number of brave schools have implemented NHA at all levels, requiring that everyone – teachers, librarians, therapists, custodial workers, bus drivers – learn and use the approach. Not surprisingly, these are the schools that reap the most benefit, most quickly.

As more educators on a particular campus commit to learning and using the Approach, campus climate shifts quickly and dramatically. Academically and socially disengaged children lean back in. Disciplinary referrals, suspensions and expulsion rates drop off the map. As children come to see one another in greatness, bullying drops off sharply, usually becoming negligible.

This simple relationship curriculum has profound impact on every child and on the teachers, administrators, and school staff members who might otherwise burn out, leave the profession, or expend massive amounts of energy being stressed and anxious about the next disruption or the next challenging child. The NHA is a powerful shortcut to enhanced emotional intelligence and social connectedness on any campus.

Punitive disciplinary methods don't work. They don't improve school climate or enhance the learning of students. In addition, recent research has uncovered shocking inequities in terms of the harshness of punitive discipline. In the U.S., a black or Latino child is much more likely to be suspended or expelled than a white child for the same types of offenses. Implementing an approach to prevent disciplinary problems is the clear solution, and the NHA has a considerable success record already:

- At Tolson Elementary in Tucson, AZ, former principal Dr. Maria Figueroa implemented the NHA school-wide. Before implementing NHA, the school had eight times the number of suspensions as the next worst in its category (including over 60 other elementary schools). Since NHA implementation, only one child has been suspended twice; no children have been diagnosed with ADHD; and no new children have been placed on medications due to behavior issues. In the years that Dr. Figueroa led Tolson, the need for Special Education services dropped from an existing level of over 15% to less than 2%. In that same ten year period of time teacher attrition dropped from initial epidemic proportions to nearly zero.

- Also in Tucson, the Head Start Early Childhood Development program implemented the NHA in 1999. The program's many intense students and chaotic classrooms responded well and quickly as teachers implemented NHA class-wide throughout the city's program sites. It dramatically improved their ability to help at-risk children do well within the classroom without needing outside services; and of 3,000 underprivileged children served since NHA implementation, in the years that the program upheld the use of the approach, no child was subsequently sent for diagnostic assessment or medication services. (Previous rates of referral were high.)

- Rose Hardie is the principal at Zimmerman Elementary in North Dakota. In 2012, she headed up a full-school implementation of the NHA at her school. She began by having her school psychologist and social worker become certified NHA trainers who could then offer small in-services in the school. A grant came through to enable Hardie to bring in Advanced Trainer Tanya Frazier to teach the approach to the entire school staff. The approach "ties into educational leadership, transformational leadership, authentic leadership – everything I've been educated on as a principal," she says. "Before the NHA, we had a high level of office discipline referrals and violent behavior. Our first training was in October 2012, and that year, our school counselor went on maternity leave. When she came back, she didn't recognize our school!" The year before, the school had had 316 office disciplinary referrals, and the year after first implementation, there were only 53 such referrals. "We went from 100 to zero restraints in a single year. Overall, since 2012, there has been a decrease of 33 percent in disciplinary referrals... In 2015, the third year of full-school implementation, no one was sent to the office for anything but greatness." Before NHA, ten kids would be lined up in Rose's office after recess to discuss their misbehavior with the principal. Training paraprofessionals on the playground to build positive relationship with students eliminated this issue. Academic achievement has improved enough in this student body (where 50% qualify for free or reduced lunch) that they've shifted from North Dakota state standards to Common Core – an indication of increased academic rigor. And, finally, while special education referrals were common before NHA, there have been no referrals for special education services in the last couple of years at Zimmerman.

- At North Educational Center in Minneapolis, MN – a special-needs school to which students with serious behavior issues are referred from 12 member districts – listening comprehension skills improved by 1.5 years over the course of a year after former principal Amy Sward implemented the NHA school-wide. North was able to reduce its School Resource Officer hours from full-time to part-time and to eliminate its time-out room; teachers complained that they were running out of curriculum because they had so much more time to teach without constant disciplinary issues.

- At the Warren County Learning Center, a special education facility in Franklin, OH, principal Pam Harsacky chose to implement the NHA facility-wide. Its 63 students, in grades 1-12, have mental health disorders, autism, and other issues, but with the NHA, the cost of running the program fell from $1,100 per month per child in 2001 to $167 per child per month in 2010. The approach has dramatically helped to keep these children in their homes and out of residential/foster placements and hospitals.

- Two foster agencies – the Drenk Center in New Jersey (now part of Legacy Treatment Services) and Focus On Youth in Ohio – implemented the NHA, teaching it to staff and foster parents to try to reduce the rate of broken placements and utilization of medications. At the Drenk Center, broken placements fell from 20-25% (before NHA) to zero (after NHA implementation in 2007). At Focus on Youth, broken placements fell dramatically and medication use dropped by 18 percent. Before NHA, foster parents working through Focus on Youth remained foster parents for an average of two years; with NHA, that length of time increased to 5+ years.

At this writing, multiple studies are in process to establish a stronger evidence base for the approach in treatment, schools and beyond.

At the NHA website (childrenssuccessfoundation.com) educators can find multiple resources, including information on how the approach can be used in the context and collaboration with the Common Core Learning Initiatives and with the Positive Behavior Intervention and Support (PBIS) approach.

Acknowledgements

I continue to be in awe of the development of the Nurtured Heart Approach. This work has gone so far beyond the confines of my original dream – both by way of the great work of the Nurtured Heart Institute and through the amazingly talented and dedicated people who continue to bring this work to their organizations, communities, classrooms and families globally.

I am forever grateful to Melissa Lowenstein, who made creating this book an absolute pleasure. Our adventures in writing continue to unfold in mysterious and surprising ways and continue to inspire. In the case of this workbook, we were dedicated to achieving the highest level of user-friendliness and support to the reader, as well as a beautiful representation of all the Nurtured Heart Approach has to offer.

When it came to birthing the book into existence, we had the great talents of Owen DeLeon – a brilliant designer who developed the concepts we had in mind beyond my wildest dreams. You are so dedicated to your craft, Owen, and your skillsets are vast. You are an absolute pleasure always to collaborate with and you are so appreciated.

Thank you so much to my beloved daughter Alice Glasser for the artwork that has become the cover and the new face of NHA. The original *Transforming the Difficult Child* book had a cover art of her first watercolor, done at the age of seven. When Alice sat me down a few years ago to pitch her idea for a new cover for the revised version of that same book, she wisely noted that since a seven-year-old may not really be fully capable of having given permission for that original art, it was time to have the real art of a now highly-trained graduate of the Rhode Island School of Design. The cover of this workbook, created by Alice and brought to graphic reality by Owen, reflects the versatility of that new image. Thank you to Freddy Mendoza for your culturally sensitive revision of the $2 ticket story.

Lastly, thank you always and endlessly to the parents, educators and treatment professionals who willingly take the Nurtured Heart Approach into the most volatile and vulnerable settings to directly benefit children. I hope the Nurtured Heart Approach continues to serve your cause. Thank you, too, to the angels who have constantly whispered in my ear sweet words of advice about ways to further cultivate and fine-tune this approach And a great appreciative thank you to Sagara Sanchez-Reinoso for bringing the Nurtured Heart Foundation into existence. You can find more at NurturedHeartFoundation.org

—Howard Glasser

I wish to acknowledge Howard Glasser and whatever otherworldly force pushed the Nurtured Heart Approach into existence through him. Howie: thank you for trusting me as your 'book midwife' and for being one of my very dearest friends. This work has supported me in parenting and working with youth in a way that completely aligns with my values and highest aspirations for their well-being and overall magnificence. Thank you, thank you, thank you.

Thank you to Jennifer Freed and Rendy Freedman for giving me an opportunity to walk my Nurtured Heart talk in your brilliant program for teens.

Thank you to my tribe of ecstatic dancers, self-help junkies, seekers, artists, and educators, including those I've come to know through Nurtured Heart. You are all absolutely amazing.

Many thanks to my family and all they have taught and continue to teach me. This includes the whole far-flung lot of them: parents, siblings, children, step-children, exes, sister-wives (that's you, Amanda Lake!) and current loves. Thanks for playing with me in the laboratory of intimate relationship and for tolerating being part of my ongoing, real-time research into getting and staying connected.

— Melissa Lynn Lowenstein Block

About the Authors

HOWARD GLASSER

Howard Glasser is the Chairman of the Board of the Children's Success Foundation and creator of the Nurtured Heart Approach. He is dedicated to awakening the greatness in all children, with a particular focus on intense and challenging children.

The approach's core methodologies, born out of his extensive clinical work, effectively inspire difficult children to successfully channel their intensity. Worldwide, hundreds of thousands of parents, educators, and treatment and child-advocacy agencies have used this approach with consistently transformative results.

Howard is the author of *Transforming the Difficult Child*, currently the top-selling book on ADHD; *Notching Up the Nurtured Heart Approach: The New Inner Wealth Initiative*, a leading book on school interventions; *All Children Flourishing*, on using the NHA with all children, difficult or not; and *Igniting Greatness*, a book on the use of the Nurtured Heart Approach as a self-care and personal growth methodology.

Four of Howard's eight books are in the top one percent of all books on Amazon, confirming the need and relevance of his message and methodology. All parents and educators, even those with well-behaved children, can benefit from learning how to inspire thriving relationships through the Nurtured Heart Approach.

Howard has been called one of the most influential living persons working to reduce children's reliance on psychiatric medications. His work also supports children in resisting addictive substances. He has been a featured guest on CNN, a consultant for *48 Hours,* and was recently featured in *Esquire.* He currently instructs educators, parents and therapists through live presentations and Internet-based courses.

MELISSA LOWENSTEIN

Melissa Lowenstein (formerly Block) is a freelance writer and editor who has written, co-authored and ghostwritten over 25 books. She has collaborated with Howard on Nurtured Heart books since 2005. She is a certified NHA trainer, a yoga teacher and student, and budding psychological astrologer; she is also a facilitator and grant writer for a program serving at-risk youth.

Nurtured Heart Approach Resources

The Nurtured Heart Institute website has an online learning center that is a ever-expanding resource center of creative applications of the Nurtured Heart Approach. Its purpose is to fill gaps in the depth and breadth of this work as well as to inspire and encourage you in this journey of gaining expertise.

The platform is called Great Voices of the Nurtured Heart Approach and can be found at **NurturedHeartInstitute.com.** There, parents, educators and treatment professionals can learn about the approach and then continually hone their expertise through innovative web courses, learning modules, discussion forums, and NHA-related research. The site also features articles, products and services supporting the approach.

BOOKS ON THE NURTURED HEART APPROACH

Books can be ordered online through Amazon.com or phone orders can be made by calling our Distributor and Fulfillment Center, Brigham Distribution, at 415-723-6611.

Transforming the Difficult Child: The Nurtured Heart Approach
(Revised 2016) by Howard Glasser and Jennifer Easley

All Children Flourishing—Igniting the Greatness of Our Children
(2008) by Howard Glasser with Melissa Lynn Lowenstein

Transforming the Difficult Child: True Stories of Triumph
(2008) by Howard Glasser and Jennifer Easley

ADHD Without Drugs—A Guide to the Natural Care of Children with ADHD
(2010) by Sanford Newmark, MD

Notching Up the Nurtured Heart Approach—The New Inner Wealth Initiative
for Educators (2011) Howard Glasser and Melissa Lynn Lowenstein

Igniting Greatness: Remembering Who We Really Are Through the Nurtured Heart Approach (2015) Howard Glasser and Melissa Lynn Lowenstein

AUDIO VISUAL RESOURCES

Transforming the Difficult Child DVD—(2004)
6 hours based on an actual filmed one-day seminar, with video clip illustrations

Transforming the Difficult Child DVD—(2004)
4 hours based on an abbreviated version of the above

Transforming the Difficult Child CD—(2011)
3.5 hours recorded from a live seminar

Transforming the Difficult Child: The Nurtured Heart Approach—available on Audible—(2023) by Howard Glasser and Jennifer Easley, read by Howard Glasser

Other titles by Nurtured Heart Approach trainers can be found at the Nurtured Heart Approach bookstore.

NURTURED HEART FOUNDATION

The Nurtured Heart Foundation is dedicated to the mission of cultivating Inner Wealth for all with a steadfast commitment to globally sharing the abundant applications of the Nurtured Heart Approach.

More can be found at NurturedHeartFoundation.org